CW00969460

Published by

THE BIBLE FOR TODAY PRESS
900 Park Avenue
Collingswood, New Jersey 08108
U.S.A.

2nd Printing
March, 2001

ISBN #1-56848-011-3

ACKNOWLEDGMENTS

I wish to acknowledge the assistance of the following people:

- **Yvonne S. Waite**, my wife, who encouraged the reprinting of the book, read the manuscript, and gave helpful suggestions;
- **Daniel S. Waite**, our son and the Assistant to the Bible For Today Director, who read the manuscript and offered helpful suggestions, and who brought up-to-date the quotations from previous editions of *Which Bible* and *Believing Bible Study* so that they would match, wherever possible, the pages of the current editions of those books; and
- **Mike Woodland**, the one in charge of our shipping department, who read the manuscript and offered helpful suggestions.
- **Mrs. Polly Freholm,** a faithful volunteer secretary, now with the Lord, who re-typed the original 1971 manuscript to make the words easier to read.

FOREWORD

- **A Revision of a 1971 Book**. This book, *The Case for the Received Text of Hebrew and Greek Underlying the King James Bible: A Summary of the Evidence and Argument,* was originally published June 25, 1971. It was my very first study on this theme. It arose out of the careful reading of three books: (1) *Which Bible* by Dr. David Otis Fuller; (2) *Believing Bible Study* by Dr. Edward F. Hills; and (3) *God Wrote Only One Bible* by Jasper James Ray.

- **A Serious Error**. In 1971, 27 years ago, this subject was new to me and I was new to this subject. I was convinced, however, that a real battle was beginning to take shape over the Bible. After reading these books, I knew which side I had to be on. I had been trained in Greek at the Dallas Theological Seminary and at the University of Michigan before that, to be on the Westcott and Hort critical textual false side of this issue. I had to admit that I had been trained to believe what I now realize was a serious error.

- **A Simple Summary**. In order to reach the most people in the simplest manner, I determined, in 1971, to make a *Summary of the Evidence and Argument* relating to the King James Bible and its underlying Hebrew and Greek texts. This is what it was--a summary.

- **An Amazing Insight**. Between 1971 and 1998, I have written many and accumulated over 1,000 titles of all types on this subject. They are available to those who are interested. After I re-read my 1971 summary I was amazed at the insight and help it contained. I have edited it slightly, and in its new format, I hope it might be even more persuasive to those who read it.

Sincerely yours for God's Words,

D. a. Waite

Rev. D. A. Waite, Th.D., Ph.D.
Director, The Bible For Today, Incorporated

THE BIBLE

"Majestic, eternal, immutable BOOK,
Inspired, inerrant, complete.
The Light of my path as I walk on life's way,
The Guide and the Lamp to my feet.

Its writings are holy and verbally true,
The unalterable Statute of Light,
For profit, for doctrine, for correction, reproof,
Infallible Guide to the right.

My Treasure, my Comfort, my Help, and my Stay,
Incomparable Measure and Rod,
Each page is replete with its textual proof,
The Bible, the exact WORD OF GOD!

By Gertrude Grace Sanborn
September, 1979,

Table of Contents

CHAPTER III
THE TRADITIONAL (OR RECEIVED) TEXT
UNDERLYING THE KING JAMES BIBLE 17

CHAPTER I
INTRODUCTORY COMMENTS

[Note: The original book was written by the author in 1971. This is a revised edition of the original material. Though much has taken place from 1971 to 1998 in the battle for our Bibles, I believe this summary of the subject will be helpful for you as well. For this reason, we feel it is important to make it available in this new and up-dated format. DAW]

I. The Writer's Qualifications and Interest in the Subject.

The present book has been written due to the writer's interest in two areas: (1) The first is the run-away explosion of new versions and perversions with a concurrent depreciation and ridicule of the King James Bible. This is indeed a grave and serious situation. (2) The second is the writer's own background in the Biblical languages which prepared him to undertake a full-scale defense of the King James Bible (and its underlying Hebrew and Greek texts) coupled with a massive attack on the new versions and perversions of our day. This preparation and scholastic background is deemed important and essential in order to be effective in this battle for God's truth.

Without appearing to be boastful, yet in the interests of factual background of the writer, the following is included in these introductory comments. This will enable readers to judge for themselves the preparation of the writer which qualifies him to express his opinions on this subject. Transcripts of the credits mentioned below are available for anyone who might be interested in them and would like to order them from The Bible For Today, Incorporated.

The writer was thoroughly prepared and trained in the original Biblical languages of Hebrew and Greek. He received credit in these languages either at the University of Michigan (1945-48) or at the Dallas Theological Seminary (1948-53) as follows: In Greek, 66 semester hours; in Hebrew, 25 semester hours; a total of 91 semester hours in combined Biblical languages. In addition to these 91 semester hours, the author has received credit for 27 additional hours in other foreign languages, divided as follows: Latin, 8 semester hours; French, 8 semester hours; Spanish, 11 semester hours. The grand total of languages, in terms of semester hours, in addition to the many other related courses taken at schools for work on the author's A.B., M.A., Th.M., Th.D., and/or Ph.D. has been 118 semester hours in languages. This is only 2 semester hours short of a solid 4 year undergraduate course consisting of 120 semester hours required for graduation in most universities today. Four of the five residency-earned degrees mentioned above (M.A., Th.M., Th.D., and Ph.D.) required research theses and/or dissertations which prepared him to deal satisfactorily with documentation and evidence.

Whatever other differences the modern critics of the King James Bible and its underlying Hebrew and Greek texts might have with this writer, they cannot justifiably criticize his preparation and training in these essential disciplines.

II. Life in a Revolutionary Age

Today we are facing a world in REVOLUTION. A "revolutionary" seeks to disrupt and/or discard a present system in order to replace it with a new and different system.

In discussing the Hebrew and Greek texts which should be used today as a basis for Bible translation here at home or on the mission fields of the world, there is a tendency also to be "REVOLUTIONARY." There is an increasing attempt to scuttle and otherwise undermine the KING JAMES BIBLE (KJB) and its underlying Hebrew Masoretic text and the Greek *Textus Receptus*. This has been done for many decades. In the past, it was done only by the liberals and apostates. In recent decades, the attacks have also come from the neo-evangelicals and even some of the fundamentalists. They have sought to throw out these verities and replace them with false substitutes. These REVOLUTIONARY actions must be resisted by every proper means, regardless of the costs involved. There is **NOTHING** more important than our Bible.

III. Preserving the Hebrew and Greek Texts

Fundamentalists should be desirous of preserving and conserving the basic English King James Bible and its underlying Hebrew and Greek texts. They should also desire to have a faithful Bible translation into every language under heaven. To do this, however, we must have an accurate and reliable Hebrew and Greek text from which to translate and reliable techniques of translation as well.

On some of these points those who call themselves fundamentalists might simply have to agree to disagree. There might come a time (perhaps it has now arrived in 1998) to take another course of action. It means that those who want to preserve the KING JAMES BIBLE and its underlying Hebrew and Greek texts [the Old Testament Masoretic Hebrew and the New Testament *Textus Receptus* Greek] will have to do battle with those who want either to destroy these historical documents entirely or else emend them into ineffectiveness. This battle must be based upon the facts in this issue. Hence, this summary of the evidence and arguments. For more than 1,000 titles defending the King James Bible and its underlying Hebrew and Greek texts, the reader is referred to **B.F.T. Brochure #1** which is available, upon request, from The Bible for Today, 900 Park Avenue, Collingswood, New Jersey 08108 USA.

IV. The Work of Translation

After the basic Hebrew and Greek texts are arrived at and agreed upon, however, it is also essential that the translations from them be as accurate, as literal (yet literary), as grammatically acceptable, and as sound a reflection of the original languages themselves as is humanly possible. Such translations, it is believed by this author, should only be made by those who have pledged themselves to the highest possible view of Scripture, namely, that the Bible in the autographs, or original manuscripts themselves as written, is the product of plenary and verbal inspiration (2 Timothy 3:16-17), and are hence both inerrant and infallible in all matters of which it speaks.

There must also be a belief in God's promise and fulfillment in the preservation of His Hebrew and Greek Words down to the present day.

V. Divisions on What Hebrew and Greek Texts to Use

The modernists and the Roman Catholics are not divided very much on their text to be used in the Hebrew and Greek. Most of the neo-evangelicals are not divided either, choosing, for the most part, to accept the text which is acceptable to the liberals and apostates in the religious world of the National and World Councils of Churches. In the Old Testament, this is the false *Biblia Hebraica* either of the Rudolf Kittel or the Stuttgartensia variety. In the New Testament, this is the false Greek text known as the Westcott and Hort text. Today, it is most commonly known as the false Nestle-Aland (26th or 27th editions) or the United Bible Societies (3rd or 4th editions) Greek text. All three of these Greek texts are based on the false Vatican ("B") and Sinai ("Aleph") Gnostic Greek manuscripts.

There is a distinct cleavage on this issue among even fundamentalists as to the Hebrew and Greek texts to use. Many fundamentalists, especially in recent years, have selected Westcott and Hort's "B" and "Aleph" manuscript family. It is heartening to know, however, that there are still many who side with the King James Bible, the Masoretic Hebrew text, and the *Textus Receptus* Greek Text underlying the KJB. We wish to aid this latter group.

VI. The Vanishing "Received Text" of Both Hebrew and Greek

The "Received Text" of both the Hebrew and the Greek Testaments, is in danger of passing off the scene. This "Received Text" refers now both to the Masoretic Hebrew Text and to the *Textus Receptus* Greek Text which is also called the Traditional Text.

A. The Masoretic Hebrew Text Being Edited

Away. In Hebrew, even the so-called "conservative" churches, Bible schools, colleges, universities, and seminaries continue to sell and use in class either Rudolf Kittel's *Biblia Hebraica*, 1950, or the *Biblia Hebraica Stuttgartensia*, 1967/77. Both of these false and erroneous editions of the Hebrew Old Testament are distributed by the AMERICAN BIBLE SOCIETY. Both of these carry in the text and in the footnotes many emendations, some of which have not the slightest manuscript evidence to justify them other than the Latin letter "L" which stands for *legendum*, ("which read"). These are dangerous editions of the so-called "Masoretic" Hebrew Bible, and should be shunned. A pure "Masoretic" Hebrew text should be sought instead, from which to base any translation of the Old Testament. Such a text is that which underlies the Old Testament King James Bible. One example of this text is called the "Letteris" Hebrew text of 1866. This was before Rudolf Kittel's *Biblia Hebraica* changed the Hebrew text in 1937. It is available from THE BIBLE FOR TODAY as **B.F.T. #2064** for a GIFT of **$50.00 +S&H**. It is a Hebrew/English parallel edition with the Masoretic Hebrew text in one column, and the King James Bible in the other column. For more information on this Hebrew text, the reader is referred to *Defending the King James Bible* (**B.F.T. #1594-P** at present, for a GIFT of $12.00 + S&H in hardback edition), Chapter II, pages 20-37 in the 5th edition.

B. The *Textus Receptus* Greek Text Today.

The *Textus Receptus*, or Received Text does not occur in most editions of the Greek New Testament today such as in the editions of Nestle, Souter, Westcott and Hort, Metzger, Aland-Black, or Metzger-Wikgren. The Nestle/Aland 26th or 27th Greek Text as well as the United Bible Societies (UBS) 3rd or 4th editions are of this variety as well. Yet these are about the only editions which are for sale in the bookstores of even our own fundamental schools, colleges, universities, and seminaries both in 1971 and in 1998. This has been the case for over 117 years now, from 1881 to 1998. These are the texts which are therefore used in the classrooms of our schools, colleges, universities, and seminaries, since they are the most readily available and also falsely presented as the best, most accurate and therefore preferred texts. These false texts are also the basis of most of the English versions and perversions of our day such as the New International Version, the New American Standard Version, the New Revised Standard Version and most of the others.

There are two editions of the *Textus Receptus* in Greek which are still in print. (1) *The Interlinear Greek/English New Testament*, by Dr. George Ricker Berry. It has an interlinear English translation under each Greek word and has the King James Bible in the margin. It uses the Greek Text of Stephens 1550, with various "B" and "Aleph" readings in the footnotes by editors as Elzevir, Griesbach, Lachmann, Tischendorf, Tregelles, Alford, and Wordsworth. There is included a Greek-English New Testament Lexicon, supplemented by a chapter elucidating the Synonyms of the New Testament, with a *Complete Index to the Synonyms*. It is by George Ricker Berry, Ph.D., of the University of Chicago & Colgate University Department of Semitic Languages. It has 811 pages. It is available as **B.F.T. #186** for a GIFT of **$30.00 + S&H**.

(2) *The Scrivener's Greek New Testament* as reprinted by the Trinitarian Bible Society. It is available as **B.F.T. #471** for a GIFT of **$14.00 +S&H**. This is the exact Greek text that underlies the King James Bible. It is only in Greek with no English at all. For more information on the issues of the New Testament Greek text, the readers are referred to *Defending the King James Bible* (**B.F.T. #1594-P** presently for a GIFT of **$12.00 +S&H** in hardback edition), Chapter II, pages 38-61 in the 5th edition.

VII. The Plan of This Paper-- Summarizing Three Basic Books

The plan of this study will be to summarize both the evidence and the argument presented from three books which deal with this subject and which are still in print. The pages used in the original 1971 edition of this study have been changed to the pages in the present editions of *Which Bible* and *Believing Bible Study*. In some instances this was not possible, and the 1971 pages were retained. The three books consulted are:

A. *Believing Bible Study* by Edward F. Hills, 1967.
The first book is entitled *Believing Bible Study* by Edward F. Hills, Th.D. It was published by the Christian Research Press, 258 pages, 1967. It is available as **B.F.T. #598** for a GIFT of **$16.00**. All of the readers of this SUMMARY should get Dr. Hills' book.

B. *God Wrote Only One Bible* by Jasper

James Ray, 1970. The second book is entitled *God Wrote Only One Bible*. It is by Jasper James Ray, Revised Edition. It was published by the Eye Opener Publishers, 122 pages, 1955 and 1970. It is available as **B.F.T. #1061** for a GIFT of **$7.50**. Its comparative studies of 44 versions and 162 key New Testament verses have real merit. All who read my SUMMARY should get a copy of Ray's book for reference and use.

C. *Which Bible?* By Dr. David Otis Fuller, 1970.

The third book is entitled *Which Bible?* It was written by Dr. David Otis Fuller. It is published by the Which Bible Publishers in Grand Rapids, Michigan. 318 pages, 1970, and other editions. It is available as **B.F.T. #169** for a GIFT of **$15.00**. Again, all who read my SUMMARY should get a copy or two of all of these books for reference and use.

D. Method of Referring to the Three Books in Quotations.

In order to save time and space, when citing one of the above three books, I will use the authors' names, followed by the page or pages of the book in question. This will include the names of Dr. Hills, Dr. Fuller, and Mr. Ray. The book by Dr. Fuller, *Which Bible*, sums up the writings of various authors.

The *Case for the King James Bible* quotes extensively from Dr. Fuller's use of the book by Dr. Benjamin Wilkinson entitled *Our Authorized Bible Vindicated*. Some of our readers might like to get the entire book to read for themselves. It is available as **B.F.T. #1123** @ **$13** +S&H. After he died, Dr. Fuller took a lot of criticism for his use of Wilkinson's book because Dr. Wilkinson was a Seventh Day Adventist. Dr. Fuller made no mention of this. When I quote from an encyclopedia I do not give the author's church affiliation, do you? I have never found any espousal of Seventh Day Adventist views throughout *Our Authorized Bible Vindicated*. On the other hand, I have found that Dr. Wilkinson had a tremendous grasp of the entire question of the issues involved in defending our King James Bible. He was severely condemned by his own church for this position. For this reason, the Bible for Today continues to offer this book. We do not necessarily agree 100% with all the authors of all the books and materials the Bible For Today offers, but we believe they are helpful in certain important areas.

Our Bible For Today ministry is opposed to the religious beliefs of Seventh Day Adventism. For those interested in this theme, you are urged to get any one or all of the following: (1) **B.F.T. #971** @ **$3** +S&H (*The Falsities of 7th Day Adventism*); (2) **B.F.T. #1998** @ **$2.50** +S&H (*Seventh-Day Adventist Church-- True or False?*); and (3) **B.F.T. #402** @ **4/$1.50** +S&H (*Why I am a Baptist and Not a Seventh Day Adventist*).

E. Why Make & "Summary of Evidence and Argument?"

The present "SUMMARY" of evidence and argument in the

issues involved in the case for the Hebrew and Greek text of the KJB is made due to the complexities involved in this subject. A little arithmetic indicates that the total number of pages involved in Dr. Edward F. Hills (258 pages), Jasper James Ray (122 pages), and Dr. David Otis Fuller (318 pages) totals 698 pages. This "SUMMARY" has confined itself to a small proportion of those pages. It highlights some of the more cogent evidence and argument presented by the various authors quoted in these volumes.

VIII. Organization of the Remainder of the Book

The remaining CHAPTERS will consist of the following themes:

CHAPTER II, A Panoramic View of Textual Matters in Hebrew and Greek.

CHAPTER III, The Traditional (or Received) Text Underlying the KING JAMES BIBLE.

CHAPTER IV, The Western Text Family of Manuscripts.

CHAPTER V, The Alexandrian Text Family of Manuscripts--"B" and "Aleph."

CHAPTER VI, Corruption in the "B" and "Aleph" Family of Manuscripts.

CHAPTER VII, Concluding Remarks.

Though the original edition of this present book (1971) made reference to the first edition of Dr. Fuller's book (1970). This present revision (1998) refers to the pages in the fifth edition (1990) of *Which Bible* by Dr. Fuller. Though it seems strange, in at least one place, the 1990 edition did not contain some quotes contained in the 1970 edition. An example of this is found on page 42. Since the quote was important, it is included in this book.

The quotations from Dr. Hills' book, *Believing Bible Study*, are as follows: for the most part, pages up to Chapter V, the third edition, 1991, pages are used. For the remainder of the book, it was difficult to find the 1991 pages, so they are from the first edition, 1967.

CHAPTER II
A PANORAMIC VIEW OF
TEXTUAL MATTERS IN HEBREW
AND GREEK

I. The Masoretic Text Is the Received Text of the Hebrew

As mentioned in the previous chapter, for a summary of the arguments concerning the Hebrew and Greek texts, the reader is referred to *Defending the King James Bible* (**B.F.T. #1594-P** presently for a GIFT of **$12.00** +S&H in the 5th hardback edition), Chapter II, pages 20-61.

Benjamin G. Wilkinson wrote:

The first stream which carried the RECEIVED TEXT IN HEBREW AND GREEK, began with the apostolic churches, [Wilkinson quoted by Dr. David Otis Fuller, *Which Bible*, p. 187]

Wilkinson also wrote:

And lastly, they contended that the RECEIVED TEXT BOTH IN HEBREW AND IN GREEK, as they had it in their day would so continue unto the end of time. [Wilkinson quoted by Dr. David Otis Fuller, *Which Bible*, p. 263]

You will note that the term "Received Text" can be applied to the Hebrew which was in existence at the time in question, as well as to the Greek text. The Hebrew text would refer to the Masoretic text that underlies the King James Bible.

A. The Hebrew Text of Christ's Day Was Reli- able. On this point, Hills wrote:

During His earthly life the Lord Jesus Christ appealed unreservedly to the very words of the Old Testament text (Matt. 22;42-45; John 10:34-36), thus indicating His confidence that this text had been accurately transmitted. Not only so, but He also expressed this conviction in the strongest possible manner. "Till heaven and earth pass, one jot or one tittle shall in no wise pass from the law, till all be fulfilled (Matt. 5:18)" . . . *Here our Lord assures us that the Old Testament text in common use among the Jews during His earthly ministry was an ABSOLUTELY TRUSTWORTHY REPRODUCTION OF THE ORIGINAL TEXT WRITTEN BY MOSES AND THE OTHER . . . WRITERS.* [Dr. Edward F. Hills, *Believing Bible Study*, pp. 6-71

For further information on Bible Preservation, see *Defending the King James Bible*, 5th edition, pages 6-19 [**B.F.T. #1594-P** presently @ $12+S&H]

B. The Masoretic or Traditional Hebrew Text was Preserved by the Jews from the First Cen- tury Until the Reformation. Hills stated:

From the end of the FIRST CENTURY UNTIL THE PROTESTANT REFORMATION THE HEBREW OLD TESTAMENT WAS PRE-SERVED not by Christians but by non-Christian Jews. [Dr. Edward F. Hills, *Believing Bible Study*, p. 12] . . .*The Amoraim were followed in the sixth century by the Masoretes* (Traditionalists) *to whom the Masoretic* (Traditional) *Old Testament text is due. These MASOR-ETES TOOK EXTRAORDINARY PAINS TO TRANSMIT WITHOUT ERROR THE OLD TESTAMENT TEXT WHICH THEY HAD RECEIVED FROM THEIR PREDECESSORS. Many complicated safeguards against scribal slips were devised, such as counting the number of times each letter of the alphabet occurs in each book . . .* [Dr. Edward F. Hills, *Believing Bible Study*, p. 13] [**B.F.T. #598/ $16**]

For further information on eight specific methods used by the Jews to preserve every letter of the Hebrew Old Testament, see *Defending the King James Bible*, 5th edition, pages 24-26.

C. Even Critics of the Masoretic Hebrew Text Agree that Rabbi Aquiba Put It in Its Final Form. Wilkinson wrote:

On the HEBREW OLD TESTAMENT, one of a group of the latest and most radical critics says: "DeLagarde would trace all manuscripts back to a single archetype which he attributed to RABBI AQUIBA, who died in 135 A.D. Whether this hypothesis is a true one or not will probably never be known; it certainly represents the fact that FROM ABOUT HIS DAY, VARIATIONS OF THE CONSONANTAL TEXT CEASED ALMOST ENTIRELY."

[Wilkinson quoting DeLagarde quoted by Dr. David Otis

Fuller, *Which Bible*, p. 263]

D. The Hebrew Received Text or Masoretic Text Was Not Even Tampered with by the English Revisers of the English Revised Version of 1881. Wilkinson stated:

By the time of Christ, the Old Testament was in a SETTLED CONDITION. Since then, the Hebrew Scriptures had been carried down intact to the day of printing (about 1450 A.D.) *by the unrivalled methods of the Jews in transmitting PERFECT HEBREW MANU-SCRIPTS. . . . Moreover, the Revisers, themselves, would have no one think for an instant that they used any other manuscripts in revising the Old Testament* [i.e. for the E.R.V. of 1881] *than THE MASORETIC TEXT, THE ONLY RELIABLE HEBREW BIBLE. Dr. Ellicott, chairman of the English New Testament Committee, repeatedly recommends* The Story of the Old Testament Revision *by Dr. Chambers. Dr. Chambers says: "The more sober critics with ONE CONSENT HOLD FAST THE MASORETIC TEXT. This has been the rule with the authors of the present revision* [that is, the E.R.V. of 1881]. *Their work is based THROUGHOUT UPON THE TRADITIONAL HEBREW. In difficult or doubtful places, where some corruption seems to have crept in or some accident to have befallen the manuscript, the testimony of the early versions is given in the margin, BUT NEVER INCORPORATED WITH THE TEXT."* [Wlkinson quoting Chambers, quoted by Dr. David Otis Fuller, *Which Bible*, p. 181]

E. Linguist and Scholar, Robert Dick Wilson, Put His Unqualified Stamp of Approval on the Masoretic Text of the Hebrew Old Testament. Henry W. Coray, in reflecting on the life and ministry of Robert Dick Wilson, a man who had mastered some *"forty-five ancient languages and dialects"* and who *"was a staunch defender of the doctrine of the VERBAL INSPIRATION OF HOLY SCRIPTURE,"* [Dr. Edward F. Hills, *Believing Bible Study*, p. 75], affirmed that Wilson accepted as accurate the MASORETIC HEBREW TEXT. Coray, quoting Wilson, wrote:

The result of those THIRTY YEARS' STUDY [wrote Wilson of his own study] *which I have given to the text has been this: I CAN AFFIRM THAT THERE IS NOT A PAGE OF THE OLD TESTAMENT CONCERNING WHICH WE NEED HAVE ANY DOUBT. WE CAN BE ABSOLUTELY CERTAIN THAT SUBSTANTIALLY WE HAVE THE TEXT OF THE OLD TESTAMENT THAT CHRIST AND THE APOSTLES HAD, AND WHICH WAS IN EXISTENCE FROM THE*

BEGINNING. [Coray, quoting Wilson as quoted by Dr. David Otis Fuller, *Which Bible*, pp. 44-45]

In a day when the *Biblia Hebraica* [Hebrew Bible] edited by both Rudolf Kittel and the Stuttgartensia edition are used, even by the most "conservative" Bible schools, colleges, and seminaries, this quote from Robert Dick Wilson is of utmost importance.

F. The Dead Sea Scrolls Also Bear Witness to the Masoretic Text of Hebrew. Hills wrote about this subject.

> *The discovery of the first Dead Sea Scroll, Isaiah A, was generally regarded by scholars as a victory for the MASORETIC* (Traditional) *HEBREW TEXT OF THE OLD TESTAMENT. M. Burrows (1948) wrote as follows: "The text of Isaiah in this manuscript is practically complete. . . and it is substantially the book PRESERVED IN THE MASORETIC TEXT. Differing notably in orthography* [spelling] *and somewhat in morphology* [form], *it AGREES WITH THE MASORETIC TEXT TO A REMARKABLE DEGREE IN WORDING. Herein lies its chief importance, supporting the fidelity of the MASORETIC TRADITION." And, according to Albright (1955), the second Isaiah scroll (Isaiah B) AGREES EVEN MORE CLOSELY WITH THE MASORETIC TEXT.* [Dr. Edward F. Hills, *Believing Bible Study*, p. 18]

II. The Approximate Numbers and Types of Greek New Testament Manuscripts in Existence Today

A. Growth in the Discovery of New Testament Greek Manuscripts and the Cataloging of Them Through The Years. As the cataloging of New Testament Greek Manuscripts became more complete, the number of Greek Manuscripts grew as follows:

Number of Manuscripts	Author or Compiler	Approximate Date
15	Stephanus (Stephens)	1550 A.D.
82	John Mill	1707 A.D.
125	J. J. Wettstein	1751-1752 A.D.
616	J.M.A. Scholz	1820-36 A.D.
3,000	F.H.A. Scrivener	1861-94 A.D.
4,000	C. R. Gregory	1884-1912 A.D.
4,411	H. C. Thiessen	1948 A.D.

4,489	Kenyon	1940 A.D.
4,969	Bruce M. Metzger	1964 A.D.
5,255	Kurt Aland	1967 A.D.

[Dr. Edward F. Hills, *Believing Bible Study*, p. 194 (1967)]

B. Thiessen's Estimate in 1948--4411 Manu-

scripts. In his book, *Introduction To The New Testament*, Fourth Edition, in 1948, Henry C. Thiessen gave the following numbers and types of extant Greek manuscripts:

170 papyrus fragments
212 uncials (capital letters, majuscules)
2,429 cursives (small letters, minuscules)
1,600 lectionaries (lesson books for public reading with N.T. extracts)
*4,411 TOTAL Number of manuscripts [Thiessen, *op. cit.*, pp. 35-51)

C. Kenyon's Estimate In 1940--4,489 Manu-

scripts. Edward F. Hills, writing in Dr. Fuller's book, quoted Kenyon, in 1940, as having the following numbers and types of extant Greek manuscripts:

170 papyrus fragments (dating from the 2nd to the 7th centuries)
212 uncials (capital letters, majuscules, dating from 4th to 10th centuries)
2,429 cursives (small letters, minuscules, from 9th to 16th centuries)
1,678 lectionaries (lesson books for public reading with N.T. extracts)
*4489 TOTAL NUMBER OF MANUSCRIPTS [Hills quoting Kenyon quoted by Dr. David Otis Fuller, *Which Bible*, p. 89]

D. Metzger's Estimate In 1964--4969 Manu-

scripts. Bruce M. Metzger, in 1964, found the Following numbers and types of extant Greek manuscripts:

76 papyrus fragments
250 uncials (capital letters, majuscules)
2,646 cursives (small letters, minuscules)
1,997 lectionaries (lesson books for public reading with N.T. extracts)
*4969 TOTAL NUMBER OF MANUSCRIPTS [Metzger quoted by Dr. Edward F. Hills, *Believing Bible Study*, pp. 39-40)

E. Aland's Estimate in 1967--5,255 Manu-

scripts. Zane C. Hodges, a former Professor at Dallas Theological Seminary, writing in Dr. Fuller's book, quoted Kurt Aland as having the following numbers and types of extant Greek manuscripts:

81 papyrus fragments
267 uncials (capital letters, majuscules),
2,764 cursives (small letters, minuscules)
2,143 lectionaries (less books for public reading with N.T. extracts)
*5,255 TOTAL NUMBER OF MANUSCRIPTS [Hodges quoted by Dr. David Otis Fuller, *Which Bible*, p. 26]

As of this revision (1998), Kurt Aland has found a 100 or so more manuscripts, but it is assumed that the percentage in each category would remain in about the same proportion. It is important to keep in mind that, as of 1967, there were in our possession at least these 5,255 MANUSCRIPTS IN THE GREEK NEW TESTAMENT, in whole or in part, and NOT merely TWO MANUSCRIPTS, namely, "B" and "Aleph" which Westcott and Hort and those who follow them rely upon almost to the exclusion of the other 5,253.

III.   Textual Matters in General

A. Critical Apparatus of Some Kind is Necessary to Show Variant Readings. Hills wrote:

Modern scholars who attempt this [that is, blending three or four or five older texts in Greek into one] *usually construct a CRITICAL APPARATUS by comparing ALL THE DOCUMENTS with one standard, printed text* [in Greek, that is] *and noting the VARIANT READINGS.* [Dr. Edward F. Hills, *Believing Bible Study*, p. 170 (1967)]

It is the thesis of this study that this end could best be achieved by using the *Textus Receptus* as the basic Greek text. It is a longer, more inclusive text than the one used by Westcott and Hort and company [i.e. "B" and "Aleph"]. The Masoretic Hebrew Text that underlies the King James Bible should be used in this same way in the Hebrew Old Testament.

B. Westcott and Hort's Absence of Many Foot- notes was Tragic and Indicated They Thought They had the "True Text," Thus Rejecting the MAJORITY of Manuscript Evidence. Herman C. Hoskier, the author of *Codex B and Its Allies--A Study and An Indictment*, [**B.F.T. #1643 @ $46+S&H**] quoted Dr. Salmon as reported in Dr. Fuller's book, said of Westcott and Hort's arrogance in this matter:

I charge Westcott and Hort with having utterly failed to produce any semblance of a "neutral" text. I charge them with the offense of REPEATED ADDITIONS to the narrative on most INSUFFICIENT EVIDENCE. I charge the Oxford edition of 1910 with CONTINUAL ERRORS in accepting Westcott and Hort's text for many verses together where THE ABSENCE OF FOOTNOTES shows that the editors consider their text as settled. [Hoskier, quoting Dr. Salmon quoted by Dr. David Otis Fuller, *Which Bible*, p. 138]

C. To be Entirely Acceptable, a Greek Text Should Record Practically EVERY VARIANT

READING of the Manuscript or Verse Being Examined.

This has not been done, however, either in the Greek text of Westcott and Hort, or in that of Souter, Nestle, or others. Hills stated:

> *Unfortunately, however, the collations of the earlier New Testament scholars were not very reliable. It was NOT CONSIDERED NECESSARY TO RECORD EVERY VARIANT READING of the manuscript that was being examined.*   [Dr. Edward F. Hills, *Believing Bible Study*, p. 195 (1967)]

This has been attempted in part in the Received Text of Stephens 1550 in the interlinear version referred to in Chapter I above.

D. Dean J. W. Burgon's Seven Tests of Truth in Weighing New Testament Manuscripts.

In his book, *The Last Twelve Verses of Mark*, Dean John William Burgon (1813-1888) was a steadfast defender of the Scriptures as the "infallible Word of God" [Dr. Edward F. Hills, *Believing Bible Study*, p. 35 (1967)]. He was also a champion of the Traditional, Byzantine, Received text of the New Testament called the *Textus Receptus* [or T.R. for short]. In his book, *The Traditional Text*, Dean Burgon defined "seven tests of Truth." Dr. Hills, quoting Dean Burgon, wrote:

> *In the end I shall ask the reader to allow that where these SEVEN TESTS are found to conspire we may confidently assume that the evidence is worthy of all acceptance, and is to be implicitly followed. A READING should be attested then by THE SEVEN FOLLOWING: (1) Antiquity or Primitiveness; (2) Consent of Witnesses, or Number; (3) Variety of Evidence, or Catholicity; (4) Respectability of Witnesses, or Weight; (5) Continuity, or Unbroken Tradition; (6) Evidence of the Entire Passage, or Context; (7) Internal Considerations, or Reasonableness. In the balances of THESE SEVEN TESTS OF TRUTH, the speculations of the Westcott and Hort school, which have bewitched millions, are "Tekel," weighed in the balances and found wanting.* [Hills, quoting Dean Burgon quoted by Dr. David Otis Fuller, *Which Bible*, p. 92; quoting Dean John William Burgon, Cf. *The Traditional Text*, pp. 28-29 which is **B.F.T. #1159 @$16+S&H.**]

On the other hand, ALL SEVEN TESTS OF TRUTH are found to be present in the Hebrew and Greek texts which underlie the KING JAMES BIBLE [Masoretic Hebrew and *Textus Receptus* Greek].

IV. The Three Types of Greek Manuscript Families in General

For the purposes of this "SUMMARY," though others classify them differently at times, some have alleged that there are three basic types or families of Greek New Testament manuscripts.**Dean Burgon denied that there were "families" of manuscripts**. He believed, as do I, that each manuscript is a solitary unit. The relationship between one manuscript and another cannot be proven, hence there can be no such thing as "families" of manuscripts. In all of his search of many manuscripts, Dean Burgon found only two or three that could positively trace their exact family ancestry. He likened the status of the Greek manuscripts to a person going into an old cemetery which had unmarked graves. There would be no possible way to determine accurately the family relationship of any of those buried there. So with the Greek manuscripts.

A. The Traditional, Byzantine, Received Text, or *Textus Receptus*. It is the thesis of this paper that this text is the closest to the original Greek autographs.

B. The Western Text--The Latin Vulgate And Others, A Much Longer Text.

C. The Alexandrian Text--"B" And "Aleph" Of Westcott And Hort, A Shorter Text. This is type of text which Westcott and Hort, the English Revisers, Nestle, Souter, Aland, Metzger, and a host of modern Greek students have accepted as the "true" Greek New Testament text as over against the Received, Traditional Text. It is the thesis of this paper to show why such is not the case.

Some add a fourth "family" to these above three--the Cesarean "family." We will not discuss this alleged "family" other than naming it since it was not mentioned in the three books being summarized.

CHAPTER III
THE TRADITIONAL (OR RECEIVED) TEXT UNDERLYING THE KING JAMES VERSION

It is the thesis of this book that this Traditional text, or the *Textus Receptus* [T.R., or the Received Text], or the Byzantine text, is the most accurate text of the New Testament available today and the closest to the original Greek manuscripts.

I. The Traditional or Received Text in General

A. A Chronology of Attempts to Corrupt the Traditional Text. In seeking to explain for himself and others the history of how the Traditional Text got corrupted, Hills postulated the following events:

1. Apostolic Age (33-100 A.D.) The original text was written by the Apostles.

2. Early Church Period (100-312 A.D.) The original text was CORRUPTED BY ALEXANDRIAN AND WESTERN SCRIBES. This was the beginning of the Western Text and the Alexandrian Text.

3. Byzantine Period (312-1453 A.D.) The original text was RECOVERED IN THE 4th CENTURY AND USED BY THE GREEK CHURCH FOR 1,000 YEARS.

4. Early Modern Period (1453-1831 A.D.) The original text was printed with slight alterations in 1516. It was USED BY ALL PROTESTANTS. It was the SOURCE OF THE KING JAMES

VERSION. [Dr. Edward F. Hills, *Believing Bible Study*, p. 184 (1967)]

B. Belief in Divine Preservation of the Bible Is As Important As Belief in Divine Verbal Plenary Inspiration of the Bible in the Original Languages.

Belief in Divine Preservation of the texts of the Bible in the original Hebrew and Greek is an essential link in the argument that leads to the conclusion that the Traditional, Received Greek and Hebrew Texts are the correct ones and closest to the original autographs. Wilkinson wrote:

> *When God has taught us that "all Scripture is given by inspiration" of the Holy Spirit and that "men spake as they were moved by the Holy Ghost," the Holy Spirit must be credited with ABILITY TO TRANSMIT AND PRESERVE INVIOLATE THE SACRED DEPOSIT. We cannot admit for a moment that the RECEIVED TEXT which, by the admission of its enemies themselves, has led the true people of God FOR CENTURIES, can be whipped into fragments and SET ASIDE FOR A MANUSCRIPT FOUND IN AN OUT-OF-THE-WAY MONASTERY [meaning "Aleph"], and for another of the same family which has lain for man knows not how long, upon a shelf IN THE LIBRARY OF THE POPE'S PALACE [meaning "B"]. Both these documents are OF UNCERTAIN ANCESTRY, OF QUESTIONABLE HISTORY, AND OF SUSPICIOUS CHARACTER. The RECEIVED TEXT WAS PUT FOR CENTURIES IN ITS POSITION OF LEADERSHIP BY DIVINE PROVIDENCE, just as truly as the Star of Bethlehem was set in the heavens to guide the wise men. Neither was it the product of certain TECHNICAL RULES OF TEXTUAL CRITICISM which SOME MEN have chosen in the LAST FEW DECADES TO EXALT AS DIVINE PRINCIPLES.*   [Wilkinson quoted by Dr. David Otis Fuller, *Which Bible*, p. 301]

C. Attacks on the KING JAMES BIBLE and the RECEIVED TEXT Which Underlies It.

1. A Period of Concerted Attack.

Some of the enemies of the KING JAMES BIBLE and therefore the RECEIVED TEXT which underlies it, were listed by Wilkinson as including: (1) "Great theological seminaries, in many lands, led by accepted teachers of learning are laboring constantly to tear it to pieces"; (2) "Catholic scholars"; (3) "other scholars who are Protestants in name" [a reference to Westcott & Hort. & company]; (4) After 1814, the "wave of higher criticism" which

> *mounted higher and higher until it became an ocean surge inundating France, Germany, England, Scotland, the Scandinavian nations, and even Russia . . . The tide of HIGHER CRITICISM was soon seen to change its appearance and to menace THE WHOLE FRAMEWORK*

OF FUNDAMENTALIST THINKING.   [Wilkinson quoted by Dr. David Otis Fuller, *Which Bible*, p. 265]

2. Specific Enemies of the King James Bible and the Texts Which Underlies It.

Other enemies of the KING JAMES BIBLE and its Hebrew and Greek texts included: (1) Simon, (2) Astruc, (3) Geddes, (4) Eichorn, (5) Semler, (6) DeWette, (who "began the work of discrediting THE RECEIVED TEXTS BOTH IN THE HEBREW AND IN THE GREEK, and of calling in question the generally accepted beliefs respecting the Bible which had prevailed in Protestant countries since the birth of the Reformation") [Dr. David Otis Fuller, *Which Bible*, p. 267], (7) Kuenen, (8) Ewald, (9) Wellhausen, (10) Griesbach, (11) Mohler, (12) Schleiermacher, (13) Coleridge, (14) Thirwall, (15) Westcott, (16) Hort, (17) Moulton, (18) Milligan, (19) Lachmann, (20) Tischendorf, and (20) Tregelles. [Wilkinson quoted by Dr. David Otis Fuller, *Which Bible*, pp. 267-274]

D. The Traditional, Received Text Triumphed for Over 1800 Years, from Its Writing Until About 1831.

Hills stated that the Traditional, Received Text, was:

> *PRESERVED during the second and third centuries mainly by the poorer, less educated Christians, mostly perhaps in the country districts and the smaller towns.   These humbler brethren, being less skillful in the use of the pen, would tend to AVOID MAKING NOTES IN THE MARGINS OF THEIR NEW TESTAMENTS and thus would KEEP THEIR COPIES FREE FROM INTENTIONAL ALTERATIONS.*   [Dr. Edward F. Hills, *Believing Bible Study*, p. 50]

Wilkinson exalted the Received Text by saying:

> *No competitor has yet appeared able to create a STANDARD COMPARABLE TO THE TEXT WHICH HAS HELD SWAY FOR 1800 YEARS IN THE ORIGINAL TONGUE, and for 300 years in its English translation, the KING JAMES VERSION.*   [Wilkinson quoted by Dr. David Otis Fuller, *Which Bible*, p. 276]

E. The Versions, Texts, Translations and Areas of the World Which Have Helped to Preserve the Traditional, Received Text Through the Years.

1. The Regions And Groups with Some Versions Listed.

The list would include; (1) The Received Text in Hebrew and Greek in the apostolic churches; (2) the church at Pella in Palestine, in 70 A.D.; [Dr. David Otis Fuller, *Which Bible*, p. 187]; (3) the Syrian Church in Antioch; (4) The Italic Church of Northern Italy of 157 A.D. [Dr. David Otis

Fuller, *Which Bible*, p. 208]; (5) The Gallic Church in Southern France in 177 A.D. [Dr. David Otis Fuller, *Which Bible*, p. 202]; (6) The Celtic Church in Great Britain in the 2nd century [Dr. David Otis Fuller, *Which Bible*, p, 196]; (7) The Church of Scotland and Ireland [Dr. David Otis Fuller, *Which Bible*, p. 197]; (8) The pre-Waldensian churches; (9) The Waldensian Churches of 120 A.D. and onward [Dr. David Otis Fuller, *Which Bible*, p. 208); (10) The Churches of the Reformation; (11) The King James Bible of 1611; (12) the Bible of the Greek Catholic Church [Dr. David Otis Fuller, *Which Bible*, p. 197]; (13) "So vast is this MAJORITY that even the enemies of the RECEIVED TEXT admit that NINETEEN-TWENTIETHS [about 95%] of ALL GREEK MANUSCRIPTS ARE OF THIS CLASS'" [Dr. David Otis Fuller, *Which Bible*, pp. 187-188.]

2. The Specific Versions Containing Mostly the Traditional or Received Text.

Hills listed various versions which contained the Received Text in the main: (1) The Peshitta Syriac Version of 150 A.D., or the 2nd century [Dr. David Otis Fuller, *Which Bible*, pp. 197-98]; (2) The Gothic Version of the 4th Century; (3) Codex W (Matthew) of the 4th or 5th century; (4) Codex A (the Gospels only) of the 5th century; (5) The "vast majority" of extant New Testament Manuscripts;" (6) The KING JAMES BIBLE of 1611; (7) Papyrus #75 [Dr. Edward F. Hills, *Believing Bible Study*, pp. 121, pp. 162-168 (1967)]; (8) Martin Luther's German Bible [Wilkinson quoted by Dr. David Otis Fuller, *Which Bible*, p. 211].

3. Some of These Versions, Being in the 2nd Century, Antedate "B" and "Aleph."

Wilkinson pointed out, as can be seen, that many of these texts or versions are dated from the SECOND CENTURY, which

> was a *FULL CENTURY AND MORE BEFORE THE VATICANUS* [that is, "B"] *AND THE SINAITICUS* [that is, "Aleph"] *saw the light of day.* [Wilkinson quoted by Dr. David Otis Fuller, *Which Bible*, p. 196]

Actually, many of these texts or versions were **TWO CENTURIES** before the 4th century Vatican and Sinai manuscripts were discovered.

II. The Traditional or the Received Text Makes up the Majority of all the Greek New Testament Manuscripts in Existence Today.

A. Hodges Estimated 80% to 90% of The Greek New Testament Manuscripts Extant

Today are of the Traditional, Received Textual Variety.

Professor Zane C. Hodges, then of Dallas Theological Seminary's staff, stated:

> It is also well known among students of textual criticism that A LARGE MAJORITY OF THIS HUGE MASS OF MANUSCRIPTS - SOMEWHERE BETWEEN 80-90% [this would be 4,200 to 4,730 out of a possible 5,255 total] - contain a Greek text which IN MOST RESPECTS CLOSELY RESEMBLES THE KIND OF TEXT WHICH WAS THE BASIS OF OUR KING JAMES BIBLE. [Hodges quoted by Dr. David Otis Fuller, Which Bible, p. 26]

My own conclusion is that the *Textus Receptus* kind of manuscripts make up, not only 80% to 90% of the total, but fully 99% of the over 5,255 manuscripts available as of 1967 (Kurt Aland's manuscript count as of that date). The detailed discussion of this 99% figure, based on Dr. Jack Moorman's book, *Forever Settled*, [available as **B.F.T. #1428 @ $21.00 +S&H**] is outlined in my own book, *Defending the King James Bible*, [hardback 5th printing, pp. 52-56 available as **B.F.T. #1594-P @ presently $12.00 +S&H**].

The footnote reference #3 cited by Hodges is from Kurt Aland, who holds to the Alexandrian Text as found in "B" and "Aleph." Yet Aland admits that "the percentage of minuscules [see Chapter II, II above] belonging to this type of text is about 90% [say, 2,400 out of 2,700], while its representatives are found also among the majuscules and later papyri." [Hodges quoted by Dr. David Otis Fuller, Which Bible, p. 26]. Hodges also stated:

> Among 44 significant majuscules described in Metzger's handbook, at least half either belong to or have affinities with THIS TEXT FORM. The low figure of EIGHTY PERCENT IS, THEREFORE, LIKELY TO BE A SAFE ESTIMATE OF THE PERCENTAGE OF WITNESSES TO THIS TEXT FROM AMONG PAPYRI, MAJUSCULES, AND MINUS-CULES TAKEN TOGETHER. [Hodges quoted by Dr. David Otis Fuller, Which Bible, p. 26]

In fact, when Aland came out with his 26th edition of the Nestle-Aland Greek New Testament Text, he used the letter "M" standing for the "MAJORITY TEXT" whenever he refers to the Traditional, Received Text. [Hodges quoting Aland quoted by Dr. David Otis Fuller, Which Bible, p. 27]

B. Wilkinson Estimated that 19/20ths [or 95%] of The Greek New Testament Manuscripts in Existence Were of the Traditional, Received Text Variety.

Wilkinson wrote;

> These manuscripts [that is, the Traditional, Received Text kind] have in agreement with them BY FAR THE VAST MAJORITY OF COPIES OF THE ORIGINAL TEXT. So vast is this MAJORITY THAT EVEN

THE ENEMIES OF THE RECEIVED TEXT ADMIT THAT NINE-TEEN-TWENTIETHS [that is, 95%] of all Greek manuscripts are of this class. [Wilkinson quoted by Dr. David Otis Fuller, *Which Bible*, p. 188]

C. Of The Thousands of Manuscripts Discovered Since The 1611 KING JAMES BIBLE, The Great Majority Are in Substantial Agreement with the Traditional, Received, Text Underly- ing the KJB.

One of the arguments against the KING JAMES BIBLE and the Received Text from which it was translated is that more manuscripts have been discovered and/or cataloged since its translation in 1611. Wilkinson answered this by writing:

It is true that thousands of manuscripts have been brought to life since 1611, but it must be emphasized that the GREAT MAJORITY OF THESE ARE IN SUBSTANTIAL AGREEMENT WITH THE TRADITIONAL TEXT UNDERLYING THE REFORMERS' BIBLES AND THE KING JAMES BIBLE. [Wilkinson quoted by Dr. David Otis Fuller, *Which Bible*, p. 250, fn. 14]

D. The Received Text Held Sway Definitely from 312-1453 A.D. and Beyond.

Hills, as quoted in Fuller, wrote:

The VAST MAJORITY of these EXTANT GREEK NEW TESTAMENT MANUSCRIPTS agree together very closely, SO CLOSELY, indeed that they may fairly be said to CONTAIN THE SAME NEW TESTAMENT TEXT. THIS MAJORITY TEXT is usually called the Byzantine Text by modern textual critics. This is because all modern critics acknowledge that THIS WAS THE GREEK NEW TESTAMENT TEXT IN GENERAL USE THROUGHOUT THE GREATER PART OF THE BYZANTINE PERIOD (312-1453). [Hills quoted by David Otis Fuller, *Which Bible*, p. 89]

Therefore, even the enemies of the Received Text admit its prevalence and predominance for these 1100 years or more.

E. The Fact That This Received Text Held Sway for so Long Attests to the Doctrine of the DIVINE PRESERVATION of the Text.

Hills, quoting Dean Burgon, tied in the unbroken chain of USE of the Traditional, Received, Byzantine Text with the doctrine of "DIVINE INSPIRATION AND PRO-VIDENTIAL PRESERVATION OF SCRIPTURE." He wrote:

The Byzantine Text, he maintained [that is, Dean Burgon], is the TRUE TEXT because it is that form of the Greek New Testament which is known to have been used in the Church of Christ in

UNBROKEN SUCCESSION FOR MANY CENTURIES, first in the Greek Church and then in the Protestant Church. And all orthodox Christians, all Christians who show due regard for the DIVINE INSPIRATION AND PROVIDENTIAL PRESERVATION OF SCRIPTURE, must agree with Burgon in this matter. For in what other way can it be that Christ has fulfilled His promise always to preserve in His Church the true New Testament text? [Hills quoted by Dr. David Otis Fuller, *Which Bible*, p. 90]

F. Zane Hodges Showed That the Received Text, Being the "MAJORITY TEXT," is The Text "NEAREST THE AUTOGRAPH" of the New Testa- ment.

Notice that Hodges uses the term, "Majority Text." In 1970, when this quote was made by Dr. Fuller, Hodges equated "Majority Text" with the "*Textus Receptus.*" In the 1980's, however, Hodges changed its meaning. He published, with Arthur Farstad, the so-called "Majority Greek Text" which differs from the *Textus Receptus* in about 1,800 places. I am opposed to this "Majority Text," but I quote references to it in the books that are being summarized. Hodges' argument went as follows:

The manuscript tradition of an ancient book will, under any but the most exceptional conditions, multiply in a reasonably regular fashion with the RESULT that the COPIES NEAREST THE AUTOGRAPH WILL NORMALLY HAVE THE LARGEST NUMBER OF DE- SCENDANTS. The further removed in the history of transmission a text becomes from its source the less time it has to leave behind a large family of offspring. Hence, in a large tradition where a pronounced unity is observed between, let us say, EIGHTY PERCENT of the evidence, a very strong PRESUMPTION is raised that this NUMERICAL PREPONDERANCE IS DUE TO DIRECT DERIVA- TION FROM THE VERY OLDEST SOURCES. In the absence of any convincing contrary explanation, this presumption is raised to a very high level of probability indeed. Thus THE MAJORITY TEXT, UPON WHICH THE KING JAMES BIBLE IS BASED, HAS IN REALITY THE STRONGEST CLAIM POSSIBLE TO BE REGARDED AS AN AUTHENTIC REPRESENTATION OF THE ORIGINAL TEXT. This claim is quite independent of any shifting consensus of scholarly judgment about its readings and is based on the objective reality of its DOMINANCE IN THE TRANSMISSIONAL HISTORY OF THE NEW TESTAMENT TEXT. This dominance has not and--we venture to suggest cannot--be otherwise explained.

It is hoped, therefore, that the GENERAL CHRISTIAN READER WILL EXERCISE THE UTMOST RESERVE IN ACCEPTING COR- RECTIONS TO HIS AUTHORIZED VERSION WHICH ARE NOT

SUPPORTED BY A LARGE MAJORITY OF MANUSCRIPTS. He should go on using his KING JAMES BIBLE WITH CONFIDENCE. New Testament textual criticism, at least, has advanced no objectively verifiable reason why he should not. [Hodges quoted by Dr. David Otis Fuller, *Which Bible*, pp. 37-38]

In explanation of the footnote #26 which he quoted, Professor Hodges stated:

This truism [that is, that the copies nearest the autograph will normally have the largest number of descendants] *was long ago conceded (somewhat grudgingly) by Hort.*

"A theoretical presumption indeed remains that a MAJORITY OF EXTANT DOCUMENTS IS MORE LIKELY TO REPRESENT A MAJORITY OF ANCESTRAL DOCUMENTS AT EACH STAGE OF TRANSMISSION THAN VICE VERSA." B. F. Westcott and F. J. A. Hort, *The New Testament In The Original Greek*, II, 45 [Hodges quoted by Dr. David Otis Fuller, *Which Bible*, p. 37, fn. #26]

III. The History of the *Textus Receptus*, or Received, Traditional Text

A. The Origin of the Term, "Textus Receptus," or Received Text.

On page "ii" in the Introduction to *The Interlinear Greek/English New Testament*, by Dr. George Ricker Berry, [mentioned above in Chapter I, VI,-- **B.F.T. #186** @ presently $25 +S&H] the following origin of the term "*TEXTUS RECEPTUS*" is given:

We have taken the Greek Text of Stephens 1550, which is the common text in this country; but as the edition of Elzevir 1624 is the one often called the Received Text, or TEXTUS RECEPTUS, because of the words, "textum . . . ab omnibus receptum," occurring in the preface (though this edition, as is manifest by its date, was NOT used for our English translation of 1611), we give the readings of this Elzevir edition in the notes, and mark them E. It is the text commonly reprinted on the Continent. In the main they are ONE AND THE SAME, AND EITHER OF THEM MAY BE REFERRED TO AS THE TEXTUS RECEPTUS. [*The Interlinear Greek/English New Testament*, by Dr. George Ricker Berry, *loc. cit.*]

B. The History of The *Textus Receptus* from Erasmus and onward.

1. Erasmus Helped in The Divine Preservation of The Bible.

Hills gave the history of how Erasmus preserved the Byzantine, Traditional, Received Text:

> *Thus as a result of this special providential guidance the TRUE TEXT won out in the end, and today we may be sure that the TEXT FOUND IN THE VAST MAJORITY OF THE GREEK NEW TESTAMENT MANUSCRIPTS IS A TRUSTWORTHY REPRODUCTION OF THE DIVINELY INSPIRED ORIGINAL TEXT. This is the text which was PRESERVED BY THE GOD-GUIDED USAGE OF THE GREEK CHURCH. Critics have called it the Byzantine Text, thereby acknowledging that it was the TEXT IN USE IN THE GREEK CHURCH DURING THE GREATER PART OF THE BYZANTINE PERIOD (312-1453). It is much better, however, to call this text the TRADITIONAL TEXT. When we call the text FOUND IN THE MAJORITY OF THE GREEK NEW TESTAMENT MANUSCRIPTS THE TRADITIONAL TEXT, we signify that THIS IS THE TEXT WHICH HAS BEEN HANDED DOWN BY THE GOD-GUIDED TRADITION OF THE CHURCH FROM THE TIME OF THE APOSTLES UNTO THE PRESENT DAY.*
>
> *A further step in the PROVIDENTIAL PRESERVATION OF THE NEW TESTAMENT was the PRINTING OF IT IN 1516 and the dissemination of it throughout the whole of Western Europe during the PROTESTANT REFORMATION. In the first printing of the Greek New Testament we see God's preserving PROVIDENCE working hiddenly and, to the outward eye, accidentally. The editor, ERASMUS, performed his task in great haste in order to meet the deadline set by the printer, Froben of Basle. Hence this first edition contained a number of errors of a minor sort, some of which persisted in later editions. But in all essentials the NEW TESTAMENT TEXT FIRST PRINTED BY ERASMUS AND LATER BY STEPHANUS (1550) and Elzevir (1633) IS IN FULL AGREEMENT WITH THE TRADITIONAL TEXT PROVIDENTIALLY PRESERVED IN THE VAST MAJORITY OF THE GREEK NEW TESTAMENT MANUSCRIPTS.*
>
> *This printed text is commonly called the Textus Receptus (Received Text). It is the text which was used by the PROTESTANT REFORMERS during the Reformation and by all Protestants everywhere for THREE HUNDRED YEARS THEREAFTER. It was from this Textus Receptus that the KING JAMES BIBLE and the other classic Protestant translations were made.* [Dr. Edward F. Hills, *Believing Bible Study*, p. 34]

In this connection, we must continue to keep in print today the "Traditional Texts" including both the pure MASORETIC HEBREW TEXT as well as the pure *TEXTUS RECEPTUS* GREEK TEXT--the texts that underlie our King James Bible. These texts must be made available throughout the world, not only in the United States of America. Furthermore, they must be made the only basis for the translation of Bibles in every language known to man. If we do not do this, it may very well be that these "RECEIVED TEXTS" of the Old and New Testaments might pass from the scene in due time, thus depriving our Christian posterity of these Divine Treasures.

Remember, those who now hold in their possession the Greek and Hebrew manuscripts of our Bibles, are either under the power of Roman Catholicism, or the Ecumenical Movement represented by the World Council of Churches or the National Council of Churches. The fundamentalists will not likely be granted access and/or possession of these copies any time soon. Our only hope is to KEEP IN PRINT copies of the MASORETIC HEBREW TEXT and the *TEXTUS RECEPTUS* GREEK TEXT while copies are still available from which to do the job.

It was the printing press used by ERASMUS that saved the RECEIVED TEXTS for the Reformation in the 16th century, and it will be the printing press used by some of us today that will save the RECEIVED TEXTS for the 21st Century and beyond--if they are to be saved at all. *". . . consider of it, take advice, and speak your minds."* (Judges 19:30d)

2. Various Versions of The Textus Receptus Delineated. Hills wrote:

One of the leading principles of the Protestant Reformation was the SOLE AND ABSOLUTE AUTHORITY OF THE HOLY SCRIPTURES. The New Testament text in which early Protestants placed IMPLICIT CONFIDENCE was the TEXTUS RECEPTUS (Received Text) which was first printed in 1516 under the editorship of ERASMUS and only slightly modified in subsequent editions during the 16th and early 17th centuries. The more important of these later editions of the TEXTUS RECEPTUS include the second edition of ERASMUS (1519), which formed the basis of LUTHER'S GERMAN VERSION, the third edition of Stephanus (1550), which is that form of the TEXTUS RECEPTUS generally preferred by English scholars, the fifth edition of Beza (1598), on which the KING JAMES BIBLE was mainly based, and the second Elzevir edition (1633), which was generally adopted on the European Continent and in which the term TEXTUS RECEPTUS first appeared. [Dr. Edward F. Hills, *Believing Bible Study*, p. 182 (1967)]

3. How Erasmus Arrived At His Greek Text Or Received Text. Wilkinson explained:

The two great families of Greek Bibles are well illustrated in the work of that outstanding scholar, ERASMUS. Before he gave to the Re-

formation the New Testament in Greek, he divided all Greek manu-
scripts into two classes: those which agreed with the RECEIVED
TEXT and those which agreed with the VATICANUS MANUSCRIPT
[that is, with "B"]. [Wilkinson quoted by Dr. David Otis Fuller,
Which Bible, p. 215]

C. The Influence of Erasmus on William Tyn- dale's English Translation of The Bible. The

Tyndale Bible was a forerunner of the Authorized, KING JAMES BIBLE and
was profoundly influenced by ERASMUS. Wilkinson remarked:

> *. . . William Tyndale is the true hero of the English Reformation. He*
> *early passed through Oxford and Cambridge Universities. He went*
> *from Oxford to Cambridge TO LEARN GREEK UNDER ERASMUS,*
> *WHO WAS TEACHING THERE FROM 1510 to 1514. . . Herman*
> *Buschius, a friend of ERASMUS and one of the leaders of the revival*
> *of letters, spoke of TYNDALE as "so skilled in seven languages,*
> *Hebrew, Greek, Latin, Italian, Spanish, English, French, that*
> *whichever he spoke you would suppose it his native tongue." . . .*
> *Across the sea, he TRANSLATED THE NEW TESTAMENT AND A*
> *LARGE PART OF THE OLD TESTAMENT. Two-thirds of the Bible*
> *was translated into English by Tyndale, and what he did not translate*
> *was finished by those who worked with him and were under the spell*
> *of his genius. The AUTHORIZED BIBLE of the English Language*
> *is Tyndale's, after his work passed through two or three revisions.*
> [Wilkinson quoted by Dr. David Otis Fuller, *Which Bible*, pp. 228-
> 229]

D. Testimonials to the Authenticity of the *Textus Receptus* or Received Text.

1. Rev. G. Vance Smith, a Unitarian Member of The English New Testament Committee Commented on the Received Text. Smith, a Uni-

tarian, was quoted by Wilkinson:

> *The Unitarian scholar who sat on the English New Testament*
> *Revision Committee acknowledges that the Greek New Testament of*
> *ERASMUS (1516) IS AS GOOD AS ANY* [He did NOT think it was the
> BEST TEXT, HOWEVER]. [Wilkinson quoted by Dr. David Otis
> Fuller, *Which Bible*, p. 245]

2. Dr. A. T. Robertson's Comment on the Received Text. Wilkinson quoted A. T. Robertson, longtime

Greek professor at the Southern Baptist Theological Seminary in Louisville,
Kentucky:

> *It should be stated at once that the TEXTUS RECEPTUS is NOT A BAD TEXT. IT IS NOT AN HERETICAL TEXT. IT IS SUBSTANTIALLY CORRECT.* [He did NOT think it was the BEST TEXT, however]. [Wilkinson quoting A. T. Robertson quoted by Dr. David Otis Fuller, *Which Bible*, p. 246]

Robertson continued:

> *ERASMUS seemed to feel that he had published the ORIGINAL GREEK NEW TESTAMENT AS IT WAS WRITTEN. . . The third edition of ERASMUS (1522) BECAME THE FOUNDATION OF THE TEXTUS RECEPTUS for Britain since it was followed by Stephens. There were 3300 copies of the first two editions of the GREEK NEW TESTAMENT OF ERASMUS CIRCULATED. His work became THE STANDARD FOR THREE HUNDRED YEARS.* [Wilkinson quoting A. T. Robertson quoted by Dr. David Otis Fuller, *Which Bible*, p. 246]

3.   Abraham   Kuyper   (1894) Commented on the Received Text. Hills quoted Kuyper as follows:

> *One of them* [that is, one of those who departed from Westcott and Hort's theories] *was Abraham Kuyper (1894), who pointed out that the PUBLICATION OF THE TEXTUS RECEPTUS WAS "NO ACCIDENT," affirming that the TEXTUS RECEPTUS, "as a foundation from which to begin CRITICAL OPERATIONS, CAN, IN A CERTAIN SENSE, EVEN DESERVE PREFERENCE."* [Kuyper quoted by Dr. Edward F. Hills, *Believing Bible Study*, p. 140 (1967)]

IV. The History, Use, and Value of the KING JAMES BIBLE of 1611

A. Trinitarian Bible Society's Secretary, Rev. Terence H. Brown, Pointed Out The KING JAMES BIBLE Translators Believed in the "Inerrancy of the Holy Scriptures." Terence H. Brown, for many years the secretary of the Trinitarian Bible Society in England, wrote:

> *. . . they* [that is, the KJB translators] *approached the task with a REVERENT REGARD FOR THE DIVINE INSPIRATION, AUTHORITY AND INERRANCY OF THE HOLY SCRIPTURES. To them it was "God's sacred Truth" and demanded the exercise of their utmost care and fidelity in its translation.* [Brown quoted by Dr. David Otis Fuller, *Which Bible*, p. 13]

This point is most important. Translations from the original language texts of Hebrew and Greek should be by only those who have PLEDGED THEM-

SELVES TO THE HIGHEST POSSIBLE VIEW OF SCRIPTURE, NAMELY, THAT THE BIBLE IN THE AUTOGRAPHS, or original manuscripts themselves as written, is the product of plenary and verbal inspiration (2 Timothy 3:16-17), and is hence both INERRANT and INFALLIBLE in all areas of which it speaks. They should also believe in the Biblical doctrine of the Divine Preservation of those original language texts in accurate copies or APOGRAPHS. Any less of a standard, to my way of thinking, is dangerous when dealing with the Hebrew and Greek texts themselves and doing translation of the HOLY WORD OF THE LIVING GOD.

B. The Scholarship of The King James Trans- lators. Terence Brown pointed out:

Advocates of the modern versions often assume that they [that is, the KJB translators], *are the product of SCHOLARSHIP FAR SUPERIOR to that of the translators of the KING JAMES BIBLE of 1611, but this assumption is not supported by the facts. THE LEARNED MEN who labored on our English Bible were men of EXCEPTIONAL ABILITY.* [Wilkinson quoted by Dr. David Otis Fuller, *Which Bible*, p. 13]

Wilkinson agreed with Brown's assessment:

No one can study the lives of those men [that is, the KJB translators] *who gave us the KING JAMES BIBLE without being impressed with their PROFOUND AND VARIED LEARNING.* [Wilkinson quoted by Dr. David Otis Fuller, *Which Bible*, p. 258]

C. The Method Used by The King James Translators. After listing the King James Bible translators by name, Terence Brown described their method:

The most LEARNED MEN IN THE LAND WERE CHOSEN FOR THIS WORK, and the complete list shows a high proportion of men with a PROFOUND KNOWLEDGE OF THE LANGUAGES IN WHICH THE BIBLE WAS WRITTEN. Of the FIFTY-FOUR who were chosen, a few died or withdrew before the translation was started and the final list numbered FORTY-SEVEN MEN. They were divided into SIX COMPANIES, and a portion was assigned to each group. EVERYONE IN EACH COMPANY TRANSLATED THE WHOLE PORTION BEFORE THEY MET TO COMPARE THEIR RESULTS AND AGREE UPON THE FINAL FORM. They then transmitted their draft to each of the other companies for their comment and consent. A select committee then went carefully through the whole work again, and at last two of their number were responsible for the final checking. [Brown quoted by Dr. David Otis Fuller, *Which Bible*, p. 14]

Wilkinson described more details in their translation method:

The forty-seven LEARNED MEN appointed by King James to ac-

complish this important task were divided first into three companies: one worked at Cambridge, another at Oxford, and a third at Westminster. Each of these companies again split up into two. Thus, there were SIX COMPANIES working on six allotted portions of the Hebrew and Greek Bibles. Each member of each company worked individually on his task, then brought to each member of his committee the work he had accomplished. The committee all together went over that portion of the work translated. Thus, when one company had come together, and had agreed on what should stand, after having compared their work, as soon as they had completed any of the sacred books, they sent it to each of the other companies to be critically reviewed. If a later company, upon reviewing the book, found anything doubtful or unsatisfactory, they noted such places, with their reasons, and sent it back to the company whence it came. If there should be a disagreement, the matter was finally arranged at a general meeting of the chief persons of all the companies at the end of the work. It can be seen by this method THAT EACH PART OF THE WORK WAS CAREFULLY GONE OVER AT LEAST FOURTEEN TIMES. [Wilkinson quoted by Dr. David Otis Fuller, *Which Bible*, p. 251]

D. Conclusions on the Usefulness and Value of The KING JAMES BIBLE. We repeat the quote made above

from Professor Zane Hodges of the Dallas Theological Seminary staff [Cf. above Chapter III, II, A] on the value of the King James Bible:

It is hoped, therefore, that the GENERAL CHRISTIAN READER WILL EXERCISE THE UTMOST RESERVE IN ACCEPTING CORRECTIONS TO HIS AUTHORIZED VERSION WHICH ARE NOT SUPPORTED BY A LARGE MAJORITY OF MANUSCRIPTS. HE SHOULD GO ON USING HIS KING JAMES BIBLE WITH CONFIDENCE. New Testament textual criticism, at least, has advanced NO OBJECTIVELY VERIFIABLE REASON WHY HE SHOULD NOT. [Hodges quoted by Dr. David Otis Fuller, *Which Bible*, p. 38]

CHAPTER IV
THE WESTERN TEXT FAMILY
OF MANUSCRIPTS

1. The Western Text Family Is Usually Characterized by Additions

Hills wrote that the Western Text was usually "characterized by additions" [Dr. Edward F. Hills, *Believing Bible Study*, p. 48 (1967)] thus making it much longer than the Traditional, Received Text. Hills also wrote:

The scribes that produced the WESTERN TEXT regarded themselves more as interpreters than as mere copyists. Therefore, they made bold ALTERATIONS IN THE TEXT AND ADDED MANY INTER-POLATIONS. [Dr. Edward F. Hills, *Believing Bible Study*, p. 177 (1967)]

II. An Identification of the Western Text by Versions and Manuscript Titles

Hills, in a very effective chart, listed the WESTERN FAMILY as including the following: (1) The LATIN VULGATE of the 4th century; (2) The OLD LATIN VERSION of the 2nd Century; (3) Codex D of the 5th or 6th century; (4) Codex D of the 6th Century; (5) Codex E of the 7th century; and (6) The ROMAN CATHOLIC DOUAY VERSION of 1582. [Dr. Edward F. Hills, *Believing Bible Study*, p. 121 (1967)]

III. Jerome's Latin Vulgate Committed to the Influence of Origen

Wilkinson pointed out that:

Jerome was devotedly committed [that is, in his Latin Vulgate translation] *to the textual criticism of ORIGEN, "an admirer of Origen's critical principles," as Swete says.* [Dr. David Otis Fuller,

Which Bible, p. 218]

IV. Even Roman Catholic Scholars Point out the Many Errors of the Latin Vulgate

Wilkinson, quoting Dr. Fulke in 1583, a Jesuit Catholic scholar, where he referred to Isidorus Clarius, a monk of Casine, had this to say:

> . . . *the other, Isidorus Clarius, giving a reason of his purpose, in castigation of the said vulgar Latin translation, confesseth that it was full of errors almost innumerable; . . . And, notwithstanding this moderation, he acknowledgeth that about EIGHT THOUSAND PLACES are by him so noted and corrected."* [Wilkinson quoting Dr. Fulke quoted by Dr. David Otis Fuller, *Which Bible*, p. 221]

V. The Reformers Rejected the Latin Vulgate in Favor of the Received Text

Wilkinson stated:

> *The Reformation did not make great progress until after the RE-CEIVED TEXT HAD BEEN RESTORED TO THE WORLD. The Reformers were not satisfied with the LATIN VULGATE.* [Wilkinson quoted by Dr. David Otis Fuller, *Which Bible*, p. 222]

VI. Some of the Men Who Favored the Western Text Listed

Hills pointed out some of those favoring the Western Text Family:

> *Sanders (1926), Clark (1933), and Glaue (1954) argue for the Western Text.* [Dr. Edward F. Hills, *Believing Bible Study*, p. 188 (1967)]

CHAPTER V
THE ALEXANDRIAN TEXT
FAMILY OF MANUSCRIPTS "B"
AND "ALEPH"

The chief opponents of the RECEIVED TEXT, even among theological conservatives and fundamentalists today, are those who prefer the Alexandrian Text Family headed up by manuscripts "B" and "Aleph." A close look at the evidence and the arguments held by this group is therefore most necessary at this point.

I. An Introduction to the Alexandrian Family of Manuscripts

A. Where Manuscripts Differed, The Alexandrian Texts Preferred the Shortest Reading. Hills wrote:

> Among the Christian scribes of Alexandria developments took another turn. According to Streeter (1924), these learned Christians followed the tradition of Alexandrian classical scholarship, which was ALWAYS TO PREFER THE SHORTEST READING IN PLACES IN WHICH MANUSCRIPTS DIFFERED. The Alexandrians were always ready to suspect and reject New Testament readings which seemed to them to present difficulties. [Streeter quoted by Dr. Edward F. Hills, Believing Bible Study, p. 47]

B. The Major Alexandrian Text Family Manuscripts and Versions Listed. Hills said, by means of an effective chart, that the Alexandrian Family was the "text of an abbreviation of the original text" and included: (1) Papyrus 75 in about 200 A.D. [In Chapter III, I, E, 2, above, this Papyrus 75 was claimed for the traditional text. It is evidently

"mixed" in form] (2) Papyrus 66 in about 200 A.D., a mixed text; (3) Codex B, or VATICANUS, in the 4th century; (4) Codex ALEPH, OR SINAITICUS, in the 4th century; (5) The ENGLISH REVISED VERSION in 1881; (6) The AMERICAN STANDARD VERSION of 1901; (7) The REVISED STANDARD VERSION of 1946; and (8) The NEW ENGLISH VERSION of 1961. [Dr. Edward F. Hills, *Believing Bible Study*, p. 121 (1967)]

C. Some of the Men Who Favor The Alexandrian Text Family. Hills gave a partial list:

Westcott and Hort (1881), Ropes (1926), Lagrange (1935), and Aland (1963) favor the Alexandrian text. [Dr. Edward F. Hills, *Believing Bible Study*, p. 188 (1967)]

To this list could be added Nestle/Aland 26th and 27th editions and before, Souter, and the UNITED BIBLE SOCIETY'S RECENT GREEK TEXT of 1965 (as well as their 3rd and 4th editions), which are being used as the basis for most, if not all, of New Testament translations throughout the entire world.

II. Defects in Manuscripts "B" and "Aleph"

A. The Early Dates of "B" and "ALEPH" in the 4th Century Explained by Favorable Climate in Egypt Where They Were Found. Professor Zane Hodges, formerly of the Dallas theological Seminary staff wrote:

In the first place, all of our most ancient manuscripts [including "B" and "Aleph"] derive basically FROM EGYPT. This is due mainly to the circumstance that the climate of Egypt favors the preservation of ancient texts in a way that the climate of the rest of the Mediterranean world does not. There is no good reason to suppose that the texts found in Egypt give us an ADEQUATE SAMPLING OF TEXTS of the same period found in other parts of the world. . . It is, therefore, most likely that the text on which our MODERN TRANSLATIONS REST [that is, "B" and "Aleph"] is simply a very early EGYPTIAN FORM OF THE TEXT whose nearness to the original is open to debate. [Hodges quoted by Dr. David Otis Fuller, *Which Bible*, pp. 28-29]

B. Burgon Concluded that B" and "Aleph" Were Not Acceptable Since They Were Unsubstantiated by Facts and Argument. John William Burgon, quoted by Dr. Fuller, wrote:

"I am UTTERLY DISINCLINED TO BELIEVE," continues Dean Burgon, "so grossly improbable does it seem--that at the end of

1800 years 995 COPIES OUT OF EVERY THOUSAND, suppose, will prove untrustworthy; [that is, the Received, Traditional Text] *and that the ONE, TWO, THREE, FOUR OR FIVE WHICH REMAIN* [that is, "B" and "Aleph" and their allies]*, whose contents were till yesterday as good as unknown, will be found to have retained the secret of what the HOLY SPIRIT ORIGINALLY INSPIRED.*

I AM UTTERLY UNABLE TO BELIEVE, in short, that God's promise has so entirely failed, that AT THE END OF 1800 YEARS, much of the text of the Gospel had in point of fact to be picked BY A GERMAN CRITIC [that is, by Tischendorf] *out of a wastepaper basket IN THE CONVENT OF ST. CATHERINE* [a Roman Catholic Convent]; *and that the entire text had to be remodeled after the pattern set by a COUPLE OF COPIES* [that is, "B" and "Aleph"] *which had remained IN NEGLECT DURING FIFTEEN CENTURIES, and had probably owed their survival TO THAT NEGLECT; whilst HUNDREDS OF OTHERS HAD BEEN THUMBED TO PIECES, and had bequeathed their witness to copies made from them. . .* [Hills quoting Dean Burgon quoted by Dr. David Otis Dr. Fuller, *Which Bible*, pp. 92-93; quoting Dean John William Burgon, as found in *The Traditional Text*, p. 12 which is **B.F.T. #1159 @$16+S&H**.]]

C. It is Unreasonable that God Would Leave the Church Without His True Text for 1500 Years, if DIVINE PRESERVATION of the Text is Believed to be True, As Promised by Christ. Hills
quotes Burgon on this as follows:

They [that is, those who believe in "B" and "Aleph" as the true texts] *believe that all DURING THE MEDIEVAL PERIOD AND THROUGHOUT THE REFORMATION AND POST-REFORMATION ERA THE TRUE NEW TESTAMENT TEXT WAS LOST and that it was not regained until the middle of the nineteenth century, when Tischendorf discovered it in the SINAITIC manuscript ALEPH, and Westcott-and Hort found it in the VATICAN manuscript B. Such inconsistency, however, is bound to lead to a SKEPTICISM which deprives the New Testament text of all authority. IF we must believe that the TRUE NEW TESTAMENT TEXT WAS LOST FOR FIFTEEN HUNDRED YEARS, how can we be certain that it has now been found? What guarantees have we that either B or Aleph contains the true text? How can we be sure that Harris (1908), Conybeare(1910), Lake (1941), and other RADICAL CRITICS are not correct in their suspicions that the true New Testament text has been LOST BEYOND POSSIBILITY OF RECOVERY?* [Hills quoted by Dr. David Otis Dr. Fuller, *Which Bible*, pp. 94-100]

D. The Holy Spirit Was And Is Able to Guard the Biblical Text in Preservation. Dean Burgon again

stated as quoted by Hills:

Burgon, therefore, was right in utterly rejecting the claims of Tischendorf (1815-74), Tregelles (1813-75), Westcott (1825-1901), Hort (1828-92), and other contemporary scholars, who insisted that as a result of their labors THE TRUE NEW TESTAMENT TEXT had at last been discovered after having been lost for well nigh FIFTEEN CENTURIES. "And thus it would appear," he remarks ironically, "that the Truth of Scripture has run a very narrow risk of being lost forever to mankind. Dr. Hort contends that it more than half lay 'perdu' [French for "lost"] on a forgotten SHELF IN THE VATICAN LIBRARY;--Dr. Tischendorf that it had been DEPOSITED IN A WASTEPAPER BASKET IN THE CONVENT OF ST. CATHERINE AT THE FOOT OF MOUNT SINAI;--from which he rescued it on the 4th of February 1859;--neither, we venture to think, a very likely circumstance. We incline to believe that THE AUTHOR OF SCRIPTURE HATH NOT BY ANY MEANS SHOWN HIMSELF SO UNMINDFUL OF THE SAFETY OF THE DEPOSIT, as these distinguished gentlemen imagine." [Hills quoted by Dr. David Otis Dr. Fuller, *Which Bible*, p. 100; partially quoting Dean John William Burgon, in *The Traditional Text*, p. 12 which is **B.F.T. #1159** @$16+S&H.]

E. Burgon Held to a Bible Divinely Inspired And Providentially Preserved And Rejected the "Naturalistic Method" of Westcott and Hort. Hills

quoted Dean Burgon again:

We see here the fundamental difference between Burgon's approach to the problem of the New Testament text and that adopted by his contemporaries, especially Westcott and Hort. In matters of textual criticism, at least, THESE LATTER SCHOLARS FOLLOWED A NATURALISTIC METHOD. They took particular pride in handling the text of the New Testament just as they would the text of any other ancient book. "For ourselves," Hort declared, "we dare not introduce considerations which could not reasonably be applied to other ancient texts, supposing them to have documentary attestation of equal amount, variety, and antiquity."

Burgon, on the other hand, followed a consistently Christian method of New Testament textual criticism. He believed that the New Testament had been DIVINELY INSPIRED AND PROVIDENTIALLY PRESERVED, and when he came to the study of the New Testament text, he did not for one instant lay this faith aside. On the contrary, he

regarded the Divine Inspiration and PROVIDENTIAL PRESERVA-
TION OF THE NEW TESTAMENT as two fundamental facts which
must BE TAKEN INTO ACCOUNT IN THE INTERPRETATION OF
THE DETAILS OF NEW TESTAMENT TEXTUAL CRITICISM, TWO
BASIC VERITIES WHICH MAKE THE TEXTUAL CRITICISM OF
THE NEW TESTAMENT DIFFERENT FROM THE TEXTUAL
CRITICISM OF ANY BOOK. [Hills quoted by Dr. David Otis Dr.
Fuller, *Which Bible*, pp. 101-102]

F. Burgon's Major Criterion Was the Question of the Numbers of Manuscripts Which Agree with Each Other. Dean Burgon, quoted by Dr. Fuller,
wrote:

Strange as it may appear, it is undeniably true, that the whole of the
controversy may be reduced to the following narrow issue: DOES
THE TRUTH OF THE TEXT OF SCRIPTURE DWELL WITH THE
VAST MULTITUDE OF COPIES, UNCIAL AND CURSIVE, CON-
CERNING WHICH NOTHING IS MORE REMARKABLE THAN THE
MARVELOUS AGREEMENT WHICH SUBSISTS BETWEEN THEM?
OR is it rather to be supposed that the truth abides exclusively with a
VERY TITTLE HANDFUL OF MANUSCRIPTS [that is, "B" and
"Aleph" and their allies], *which at once DIFFER FROM THE GREAT*
BULK OF WITNESSES, AND strange to say--ALSO AMONGST
THEMSELVES. [Dr. David Otis Dr. Fuller, *Which Bible*, pp. 125-
126; quoting Dean John William Burgon, in *The Traditional Text*, pp.
16-17].

G. Burgon Believed Manuscript Evidence Should Be Decided by the Bulk of the Manuscripts in Existence, NOT by a Slim Minority of those Manuscripts. Dean Burgon also stated:

That witnesses are to be weighed--not counted--is a maxim of which
we hear constantly. It may be said to EMBODY MUCH FUNDA-
MENTAL FALLACY. It assumes that the witnesses we possess are
capable of being weighed and that every critic is competent to weigh
them, neither of which proposition is true. NUMBER IS THE MOST
ORDINARY INGREDIENT OF WEIGHT. IF TEN WITNESSES ARE
CALLED INTO COURT AND NINE GIVE THE SAME ACCOUNT
WHILE ONE CONTRADICTS THE OTHER NINE, WHICH WILL BE
ACCEPTED? The nine, of course. 63 uncials--737 cursives--413
lectionaries are known to survive of the gospels alone. By what
process of reasoning can it be thought credible that the FEW
WITNESSES shall prove the trustworthy guide and the MANY

WITNESSES the deceivers? [Dr. David Otis Dr. Fuller, *Which Bible*, pp. 125-126; quoting Dean John William Burgon, in *The Traditional Text*, p. 43]

H. Burgon mentioned the Deficiency of Manuscript "B" Which Omitted Many Words, Clauses, and Sentences in the Gospels Alone.

Dean Burgon stated:

> *Codex B is discovered not to contain in the gospels alone 237 words, 452 clauses, 748 whole sentences, which the later copies are observed to exhibit in the same places and in the same words. By what possible hypothesis will such a correspondence of the copies be accounted for if these words, clauses, and sentences are indeed, as is pretended, nothing else but spurious accretions to the text?* [Dr. David Otis Dr. Fuller, *Which Bible*, p. 127; quoting Dean John William Burgon, in *The Traditional Text*, p. 78]

I. "B" and "Aleph" Are Inferior Because They Are Covered with Blots.

Dean Burgon, as quoted by Dr. Fuller, wrote:-

> *B and Aleph are COVERED ALL OVER WITH BLOTS--Aleph even more than B. How could they ever have gained the characters which have been given them, is passing strange. But even great scholars are human* [he refers to Westcott and Hort, Tregelles and Tischendorf] *and have their prejudices and other weaknesses, and their disciples follow them everywhere submissively as sheep.* [Dr. David Otis Dr. Fuller, *Which Bible*, p. 128]

J. Herman Hoskier Pointed Out 3,000 Differ- ences Between "B" and "Aleph" Themselves.

Hos- kier stated:

> *That Aleph and B occasionally (over 3,000 REAL DIFFERENCES BETWEEN ALEPH AND B ARE RECORDED IN THE GOSPELS ALONE.) are INCONSISTENT WITH THEMSELVES appears certain in several places. Carefully as B is written, now and again it presents an ungrammatical reading, which proves on examination to be the fragment of a rival variant.* [Hoskier quoted by Dr. David Otis Fuller, *Which Bible*, p. 136]

K. Dr. Scrivener Pointed Out "DEPRAVA- TIONS OF CODEX ALEPH."

Dr. Frederick Scrivener, as quoted by Wilkinson, wrote:

> *Concerning the DEPRAVATIONS OF CODEX ALEPH* [that is, Sinaiticus, found by Tischendorf in the St. Catherine Convent in the WASTEBASKET[, *we have the further testimony of Dr. Scrivener.*

In 1864 he published A Full Collation Of The Codex Sinaiticus [that is, Aleph]. *In the introductions he makes it clear that this document was CORRECTED BY TEN DIFFERENT SCRIBES "AT DIFFERENT PERIODS." He tells of "the occurrence of SO MANY DIFFERENT STYLES OF HANDWRITING, APPARENTLY DUE TO PENMEN REMOVED FROM EACH OTHER BY CENTURIES, WHICH DEFORM BY THEIR CORRECTIONS EVERY PAGE OF THIS VENERABLE-LOOKING DOCUMENT." Codex Aleph is "covered by such ALTERATIONS, brought in by at least TEN DIFFERENT REVISERS, SOME OF THEM SYSTEMATICALLY SPREAD OVER EVERY PAGE."* [Wilkinson quoting Scrivener quoted by Dr. David Otis, *Which Bible*, pp. 307-308]

III. Westcott and Hort and Other Translators of the English Revised Version of 1881

A. The English Revised Version of 1881 Changed The Received Text Used for The KING JAMES BIBLE Over 5,000 Times. Wilkinson wrote:

This Revision Committee, [that is, for the English Revised Version of 1881, ERV] *besides the changes in the Old Testament, MADE OVER 5,000 CHANGES IN THE RECEIVED TEXT OF THE NEW TESTAMENT AND SO PRODUCED A NEW GREEK NEW TESTAMENT.* [This was basically the Westcott and Hort text based primarily on "B" and "Aleph"] [Wilkinson quoted by Dr. David Otis Dr. Fuller, *Which Bible*, p. 178]

1. Everts Counted 5,337 Changes The ERV Made in the KJB Greek Text. Everts, who was quoted by Wilkinson, wrote:

So the Revisers [that is, of the ERV of,,1881] *"went on changing until they had altered the Greek Text in 5,337 places."* [Wilkinson quoted by Dr. David Otis Dr. Fuller, *Which Bible*, p. 294]

My actual count of the places in the New Testamernt where Westcott and Hort changed the Greek *Textus Receptus* is 5,604. If you add the number of Greek words that were either added to the *Textus Receptus* by Westcott and Hort's text, or subtracted or changed in some other way by them, the total is 9,970 Greek words. This is explained more fully in my book, *Defending the King James Bible*, 5th printing, hardback, pp. 41-42. It is available as **B.F.T. #1594-P** @ presently **$12.00 +S&H.**

2.   Wilkinson   Tabulated   36,000 Changes in the English ERV as Over Against The English KJB, and Almost 6,000 Changes in The KJB Greek Text. Wilkinson said:

Even the jots and tittles of the Bible are important. God has pronounced TERRIBLE WOES UPON THE MAN WHO ADDS TO OR TAKES AWAY FROM THE VOLUME OF INSPIRATION. The REVISERS apparently felt no constraint on this point, for they made 36,000 CHANGES IN THE ENGLISH OF THE KING JAMES BIBLE and very NEARLY 6,000 IN THE GREEK TEXT. Dr. Ellicott, in submitting the Revised Version to the Southern Convocation in 1881, declared that they had made between EIGHT AND NINE CHANGES IN EVERY FIVE VERSES, and in about every ten verses, three of these were made for CRITICAL PURPOSES. [Wilkinson quoted by Dr. David Otis Dr. Fuller, *Which Bible*, p. 298]

B. English Revised Version Changes Were Made Mostly Due to the Influence of "B" and "Aleph." Canon Cook, who was quoted by Wilkinson, wrote:

And for the most of these changes the VATICAN ["B"] and SINAITIC ["Aleph"] MANUSCRIPTS are responsible. As Canon Cook says: "By far the greatest number of innovations, including those which give the severest shocks to our minds, are adopted on the AU-THORITY OF TWO MANUSCRIPTS, or even of ONE MANU-SCRIPT, against the DISTINCT TESTIMONY OF ALL OTHER MANUSCRIPTS, UNCIAL AND CURSIVE. THE VATICAN CODEX ["B"] . . . sometimes ALONE, generally in accord with the SINAITIC ["Aleph"], is RESPONSIBLE FOR NINE-TENTHS OF THE MOST STRIKING INNOVATIONS IN THE REVISED VERSION." [Wilkinson quoting Cook quoted by Dr. David Otis Dr. Fuller, *Which Bible*, p. 298]

C. The Translators of The English Revised Version of 1881.

1. The Proper Qualifications for Bible Translators. Wilkinson wrote:

It [that is, the Bible] is the handiwork of God through the centuries. ONLY THOSE WHOSE RECORDS ARE LIFTED HIGH ABOVE SUSPICION CAN BE ACCEPTED AS QUALIFIED TO TOUCH IT. Certainly no living being, or any number of them, ever had authority to make such astounding CHANGES as were made by those men who

were directly or indirectly influenced by the Oxford Movement.
[Wilkinson quoted by Dr. David Otis Dr. Fuller, *Which Bible*, p. 302]
I could not possibly agree more with this sentiment, as I have already mentioned.

2. One of the Revisers of the ERV of 1881 Denied the Deity of Christ. Wilkinson wrote:

Some of those who had part in these Revised and Modern Bibles were HIGHER CRITICS of the most pronounced type. At least one man sat on the Revision Committee of 1881 who HAD OPENLY AND IN WRITING DENIED THE DIVINITY OF OUR LORD AND SAVIOUR JESUS CHRIST. On this account, their chairman of high standing absented himself from the first. [Wilkinson quoted by Dr. David Otis Dr. Fuller, *Which Bible*, pp. 178-179]

3. Specific Names of Some of the Revisers and Some of Their Views. Wilkinson pointed out:

We meet the paradox in the Revisers, as they sit assembled at their task, of men possessing HIGH REPUTATION FOR LIBERALISM OF THOUGHT, yet acting for a decade with extreme NARROWNESS: Stanley, Thirwall, Vaughan, HORT, WESTCOTT, Moverly--men of leading intellect--would naturally be expected to be so broad as to give most sacred documents FAIR CONSIDERATION. . . When Bishop Colenso, of Natal, was on trial, amid great excitement throughout all England, FOR HIS DESTRUCTIVE CRITICISM OF THE FIRST FIVE BOOKS OF MOSES, Dean Stanley [one of the Revisers] *stood up among his religious peers and PLACED HIMSELF ALONGSIDE OF COLENSO. He said: "I might mention one who . . . has ventured to say that the PENTATEUCH IS NOT THE WORK OF MOSES; . . . who has ventured to say that THE NARRATIVES OF THOSE HISTORICAL INCIDENTS ARE colored not infrequently by the necessary infirmities which belong to the human instruments by which they were conveyed--and that individual IS THE ONE WHO NOW ADDRESSES YOU. If you pronounce against the Bishop of Natal ON GROUNDS SUCH AS THESE, you must remember that there is one close at hand whom . . . you will be obliged TO CONDEMN."*

Bishop Thirwall, of "princely intellect," had a WELL-KNOWN REPUTATION FOR LIBERALISM IN THEOLOGY. He introduced both the NEW THEOLOGY OF SCHLEIERMACHER AND HIGHER CRITICISM INTO ENGLAND. In fact, when Convocation yielded to public indignation so far as essentially to ASK DR. SMITH, THE UNITARIAN SCHOLAR, TO RESIGN, BISHOP THIRWALL retired from the Committee and REFUSED TO BE PLACATED UNTIL IT WAS SETTLED THAT DR. SMITH SHOULD REMAIN. . . Dr. G.

Vance Smith, THE UNITARIAN MEMBER OF THE COMMITTEE, is well known through his book on The Bible And Theology. *This amounted practically to CHRISTIANIZED INFIDELITY.* [Wilkinson quoted by Dr. David Otis Dr. Fuller, *Which Bible*, pp. 296-297]

4. Additional Views of The ERV Revisers as a Group. Wilkinson said:

The reader must judge whose bias he will accept--that of the influence of the Protestant Reformation, as heading up in the AUTHORIZED VERSION; or that of the influence of DARWINISM, HIGHER CRITICISM, INCIPIENT MODERN RELIGIOUS LIBERALISM, AND A REVERSION TO ROME, as heading up in the REVISED VERSION. If we select the latter bias, we must remember that both HIGHER CRITICISM AND ROMANISM REJECT THE AUTHORITY OF THE BIBLE AS SUPREME. [Wilkinson quoted by Dr. David Otis Dr. Fuller, *Which Bible*, p. 303]

This is why only men who believe in verbal, plenary inspiration of the Bible and its consequent inerrancy and infallibility in the autographs [2 Timothy 3:16-17] and the preservation of those autographs should be on any translating committee today, in my judgment.

5. The Influence of Eclecticism and Gnosticism, in The ERV Revisers. Wilkinson wrote:

CARDINAL NEWMAN believed that tradition and the Catholic Church were above the Bible. WESTCOTT AND HORT, great admirers of NEWMAN, were on the REVISION COMMITTEE IN STRONG LEADERSHIP. DEAN STANLEY [one of the ERV Revisers] *believed that THE WORD OF GOD DID NOT DWELL IN THE BIBLE ALONE, BUT THAT IT DWELT IN THE SACRED BOOKS OF OTHER RELIGIONS AS WELL. DR. SCHAFF* [also an ERV Reviser] *sat in the PARLIAMENT OF RELIGIONS AT THE CHICAGO WORLD'S FAIR, 1893, and was so happy among the BUDDHISTS, CONFUCIANISTS, SHINTOISTS, and OTHER WORLD RELIGIONS, that he said he would be willing to die among them. The spirit of the Revisionists on both sides of the ocean was an effort to find the Word of God by THE STUDY OF COMPARATIVE RELIGIONS. This is the spirit of GNOSTICISM; it is not true faith in the INSPIRATION AND INFALLIBILITY OF THE BIBLE.* [Wilkinson quoted by Dr. David Otis Dr. Fuller, *Which Bible*, pp. 308-309]

D. The Heretical Theology of Westcott and Hort, The Leaders of The English Revised Version Committee and of The False Acceptance of "B" and "Aleph." Since Westcott and Hort were the two leaders

responsible for leading even present-day theological conservatives and fundamentalists into the false acceptance of the Greek Alexandrian Texts of "B" and "Aleph," it behooves us to know thoroughly some of their theological heresies and prejudices. We should then ask ourselves if such men were living today [such as many of the translators of the Revised Standard Version (RSV), its historical relative] would we who are "fundamentalists" and separatists accept their decisions in textual matters as many accept those of Westcott and Hort, who were in many respects equally liberal, modernistic, and apostate? Would we, for example, accept the textual criticism espoused by BISHOP JAMES K. PIKE? Herein lies the most crucial part of this paper as to both evidence and argument.

To the references below concerning the heresies of both Bishop Westcott and Professor Hort might be added the following available materials: (1) *The Theological Heresies of Westcott and Hort* by this writer (**B.F.T. #595 @ $3+S&H**). (2) *Bishop Westcott's Clever Denial of Christ's Bodily Resurrection* by this writer (**B.F.T. #1131 @ $4+S&H**). (3) *The Life and Letters of Bishop Westcott* by his son (**B.F.T. #1866 @ $45 +S&H**). And (4) *The Life and Letters of Professor Hort* by his son (**B.F.T. #1867 @ $48 +S&H**).

1. Westcott and Hort, the Salesmen of "B" and "Aleph," were Believers in HIGHER CRITICISM. Wilkinson cited the following:

a. Westcott's Higher Criticism.

Westcott wrote to his fiancee, Advent Sunday, 1847:

All stigmatize him [Dr. Hampden] *as a "HERETIC" . . . If he be condemned, what will become of ME! . . . The battle of the INSPIRATION OF SCRIPTURE has yet to be fought, and how earnestly I could pray that I might aid the truth in that."* [by denial of plenary, verbal inspiration and consequent inerrancy and infallibility, that is.] [Wilkinson quoted by Dr. David Otis Dr. Fuller, *Which Bible*, p. 278]

b. Hort's Higher Criticism, Especially in the Matter of the Authority Of the Bible. Hort wrote to Rev. Rowland Williams, October 21, 1858:

"Further I agree with them [authors of Essays and Reviews] *in condemning many leading specific doctrines of the popular theology. . . . . EVANGELICALS SEEM TO ME PERVERTED rather than untrue. There are, I fear, still MORE SERIOUS DIFFERENCES BETWEEN US ON THE SUBJECT OF AUTHORITY, AND ESPECIALLY THE AUTHORITY OF THE BIBLE.* [Wilkinson quoted by Dr. David Otis Dr. Fuller, *Which Bible*, p. 278]

c. Hort's Higher Criticism, Especially in the Matter of Darwinian Evolution. Hort

wrote to Rev. John Ellerton, April 3, 1860:

> *But the book which has most engaged me is DARWIN. Whatever may be thought of it, it is a book that one is PROUD TO BE CONTEMPORARY WITH. . . My feeling is STRONG that THE THEORY IS UNANSWERABLE. If so, it opens up a new period.* [Wilkinson quoted by Dr. David Otis Dr. Fuller, *Which Bible*, p. 278]

What would our fundamentalists today say to an EVOLUTIONIST on our Bible Translation Committee?

2. Westcott and Hort, the Salesmen of "B" and "Aleph," were Mariolaters. Wilkinson used the following quotations:

a. Westcott's Admiration for the Statue of Mary. Westcott wrote from France to his fiancee, 1847:

> *After leaving the monastery, we shaped our course to a little oratory which we discovered on the summit of a neighboring hill. . . Fortunately we found the door open. It is very small, with one kneeling-place; and behind a screen was a 'Pieta' the size of life [i.e. a VIRGIN AND DEAD CHRIST]. Had I been alone I COULD HAVE KNELT THERE FOR HOURS.* [Wilkinson quoted by Dr. David Otis Dr. Fuller, *Which Bible*, p. 278]

b. Hort's "Mary-Worship." Hort wrote to Westcott, October 17, 1865:

> *I have been persuaded for many years that MARY-WORSHIP and 'Jesus'-worship HAVE VERY MUCH IN COMMON in their causes and their results."* [Wilkinson quoted by Dr. David Otis Dr. Fuller, *Which Bible*, p. 279]

c. Hort's Admitted Sacerdotalism. Hort wrote to Dr. Lightfoot, October 26, 1867:

> *But you know I AM A STAUNCH SACERDOTALIST."* [Wilkinson quoted by Dr. David Otis Dr. Fuller, *Which Bible*, p. 279]

3. Westcott and Hort, the Salesmen of "B" and "Aleph," Denied The Historicity of Gen- esis 1-3, and the Real Fall of Adam.

a. Westcott's Denial of the Historicity of Genesis 1-3. Wilkinson wrote that Westcott wrote to the Archbishop of Canterbury on Old Testament criticism, March 4, 1890:

> *No one now, I suppose, HOLDS THAT THE FIRST THREE CHAPTERS OF GENESIS, for example, GIVE A LITERAL HISTORY. I could never understand how anyone reading them with open eyes*

could think they did. [Wilkinson quoted by Dr. David Otis Dr. Fuller, *Which Bible*, p. 280]

b. Hort Denied Eden and the Real Fall of Man.
Hort wrote John Ellerton:

> *I am inclined to think that no such state as 'EDEN' (I mean the popular notion) EVER EXISTED, AND THAT ADAM'S FALL IN NO DEGREE DIFFERED FROM THE FALL OF EACH OF HIS DESCENDANTS, as Coleridge justly argues."* [Wilkinson quoted by Dr. David Otis Dr. Fuller, *Which Bible*, p. 280]

4. Westcott and Hort, the Salesmen of "B" and "Aleph," Denied the Biblical Doctrine of the Substitutionary Death of Christ for Sinners.
Wilkinson gave the following quotes:

a. Westcott's Denial of Christ's "Sacrifice and Vicarious Punishment."
Westcott wrote to his wife, Good Friday, 1865:

> *This morning I went to hear the Hulsean Lecturer. He preached ON THE ATONEMENT. . . All he said was very good, but then HE DID NOT ENTER INTO THE GREAT DIFFICULTIES OF THE NOTION OF SACRIFICE AND VICARIOUS PUNISHMENT.* [Wilkinson quoted by Dr. David Otis Dr. Fuller, *Which Bible*, pp. 280-281]

b. Westcott and Hort Both Denied the Substitutionary Death of Christ for the Sinner.

> *Westcott believed that the DEATH OF CHRIST was of His human nature, not of His Divine nature, otherwise man could not do what Christ did in death. Dr. Hort agrees in the following letter to Westcott. BOTH REJECTED THE ATONEMENT OF THE SUBSTITUTION OF CHRIST FOR THE SINNER, OR VICARIOUS ATONEMENT; BOTH DENIED THAT THE DEATH OF CHRIST COUNTED FOR ANYTHING AS AN ATONING FACTOR. They emphasized atonement through INCARNATION. This is the CATHOLIC DOCTRINE. It helps defend the Mass.* [Wilkinson quoted by Dr. David Otis Dr. Fuller, *Which Bible*, p. 281]

c. Hort Called Christ's Substitutionary Atonement An "Immoral and Material Counterfeit."
Hort wrote to Westcott, October 15, 1860:

> *Today's post brought also your letter . . . I entirely agree--correcting one word--with what you there say on the ATONEMENT, having for many years believed that "the absolute union of the Christian (or*

rather, of man) with Christ Himself" is the spiritual truth of which the
POPULAR DOCTRINE OF SUBSTITUTION IS AN IMMORAL AND
MATERIAL COUNTERFEIT. . . Certainly nothing could be more
UNSCRIPTURAL than the modern limiting of Christ's BEARING
OUR SINS AND SUFFERINGS, TO HIS DEATH; but indeed that is
only one aspect of an ALMOST UNIVERSAL HERESY. [Wilkinson
quoted by Dr. David Otis Dr. Fuller, *Which Bible*, p. 281]

How can fundamentalists accept the work of Westcott and Hort in their biased
praising of the false Greek Manuscripts "B" and "Aleph" when they once realize
that these two men were nothing but APOSTATES OF THEIR DAY? It would
be as foolish and as unbiblical to accept on Biblical matters today, the statements
of APOSTATE Joseph Fletcher, APOSTATE G. Bromily Oxnam, APOSTATE
Bishop James K. Pike, or APOSTATE Hugh J. Schonfield.

E. Westcott and Hort were Leaders in a "Thorough Scheme" in The ERV Which was an "Intentional Systematic Depravation." Wilkinson

wrote:

How vastly different are the ERRORS OF THE REVISED [that is, the
ERV of 1881 in contrast to the good work of the Received Text and
the KJB of 1611] *They are the product of a WELL-LAID,*
DESIGNING SCHEME to incorporate in the text THE THEOLOGY
OF THE REVISERS. Westcott, writing to Hort before the committee
was under way [that is, the Revision Committee for the ERV],
rejoiced that the future chairman, Dr. Ellicott, was "quite capable of
accepting heartily and adopting personally a THOROUGH
SCHEME." And when the new book was published, Bishop Westcott
recommended it to the Bible student, because the profound effect on a
DOCTRINE WAS PRODUCED BY CHANGING "HERE A LITTLE,
THERE A LITTLE." He clearly convicted the REVISED VERSION of
being the PRODUCT OF A DESIGNING SCHEME WITH AN
ULTERIOR PURPOSE. He said: "But the value of the Revision
[wrote Westcott himself] *is most clearly seen when the student*
considers together a considerable GROUP OF PASSAGES WHICH
BEAR UPON SOME ARTICLE OF FAITH. The ACCUMULATION
OF SMALL DETAILS THEN PRODUCES ITS FULL EFFECT. . . All
must see that it was a "THOROUGH SCHEME." The dominant
minds on the Revision Committee approached their task, committed
be- forehand to this "THOROUGH SCHEME." The ERRORS
therefore of the REVISED VERSION are NOT INCIDENTAL AND
ACCIDENTAL, as those of the Received Text, but are so SYS-
TEMATICALLY INTERLINKED THAT THEY CONSTITUTE WITH
CUMULATIVE EFFECT VITAL CHANGES IN DOCTRINE. The

Revised Version bears the stamp of INTENTIONAL SYSTEMATIC DEPRAVATION. [Wilkinson quoted by Dr. David Otis Dr. Fuller, *Which Bible*, pp. 214-215 in the 1970 edition, but eliminated in the 1990 edition for some reason unknown to me. DAW]
The bitter fruit begun in 1881 was later brought to an even more bitter harvest in the RSV which merely carried the ERV of 1881 even further, based upon the same Greek text for the most part, i.e. "B" and "Aleph."

F. The Questionable and Sloppy, Secret Methods Used by the ERV.

There was a marked difference in method between the KJB translators and the ERV translators Wilkinson wrote:

The translators of 1611 [of the KJB, that is] *organized themselves into six different companies. Each company allotted to each of its members a series of independent portions of the Bible to translate, so that all would act as CHECKS AND COUNTERCHECKS on one another, in order that the truth might be transmitted. Above all, their inter-relations were so preserved that the world would receive the gift of a masterpiece. Their units were organizations of construction, on the other hand, the units of the 1881 Revision* [the ERV, that is] *DID NOT MAKE FOR PROTECTION AND INDEPENDENCE, BUT RATHER FOR THE SUPPRESSION OF INDIVIDUALITY AND FREEDOM AND FOR TYRANNICAL DOMINATION. The instruments of warfare which they brought to their task were NEW AND UNTRIED RULES FOR THE DISCRIMINATION OF MANUSCRIPTS* [that is, their reliance on "B" and "Aleph"]; *for attacking the verb; for attacking the article; for attacking the preposition, the pronoun, the intensive, Hebraisms, and parallelisms.* [Wilkinson quoted by Dr. David Otis Dr. Fuller, *Which Bible*, pp. 298-299]

This is the method used by altogether too many of our modern-day translations also, that is, a SECRECY and a "TYRANNICAL DOMINATION" in the translation process. Often, such as in the case of the "GOOD NEWS FOR MODERN MAN," (*Today's English Version*) only an "editor's" name appears.

G. Westcott and Hort's Undermining of the Received Greek Text Opened the Way for Trans- lations Also Based on a Faulty Text to Multiply.

Wilkinson commented:

When Doctors Westcott and Hort called "VILE" and "VILLAINOUS" the RECEIVED TEXT which, by the providence of God, was accounted an authority for 1800 YEARS, they opened wide the door for individual and religious sects to BRING FORTH NEW BIBLES solely UPON THEIR AUTHORITY, [Wilkinson quoted by Dr. David Otis Dr. Fuller, *Which Bible*, p. 310]

1. Twisted "Rules of Textual Criticism" Prevailed in These New Translations.

Wilkinson wrote:

> *How far the NEW THEOLOGY has been adopted by the EDITORS of the MANY DIFFERENT KINDS OF MODERN BIBLES, is a question space does not permit us to pursue. In the main, all these NEW EDITIONS conform to the MODERN RULES OF TEXTUAL CRITICISM* [meaning those false rules laid by APOSTATES Westcott and Hort and company]. *We have already mentioned Fenton, Goodspeed, Moffatt, Moulton, Noyes, Rotherham, Weymouth, Twentieth Century, The Polychrome, and the Shorter Bible.* [Wilkinson quoted by Dr. David Otis Dr. Fuller, *Which Bible*, p. 309]

2. The Dangers in the "Shorter Bible."

In this "Shorter Bible," the mania to SHORTEN the verses which Westcott and Hort accepted by their approval of "B" and "Aleph" Alexandrian manuscripts, was followed to its disastrous conclusion. Wilkinson said:

> *Anyone who will take the pains to secure a copy of the "Shorter Bible" in the New Testament will recognize that ABOUT FOUR THOUSAND of the nearly EIGHT THOUSAND VERSES in that Scripture HAVE BEEN ENTIRELY BLOTTED OUT.* [Wilkinson quoted by Dr. David Otis Dr. Fuller, *Which Bible*, p. 275]

IV. "B" And "Aleph" Weighed Against the Received Text of the KING JAMES BIBLE

A. An Answer to the Argument that the Copies of "B" and "Aleph" are Older Than the Copies We Now Have of the Received, Traditional Text.

Professor Zane C. Hodges, formerly of the Dallas Theological Seminary staff, wrote:

> *. . . It is almost a truism in textual research that THE OLDEST MANUSCRIPT DOES NOT NECESSARILY CONTAIN THE BEST TEXT. Still, the argument from "old manuscripts" can be presented in a way that sounds impressive. . . In the first place, all of our most ancient manuscripts derive basically from EGYPT. This is due mainly to the circumstance that the climate of Egypt favors the PRESERVATION OF ANCIENT TEXTS in a way that the climate of the rest of the Mediterranean world does not. There is no reason to suppose that the texts found in EGYPT give us an ADEQUATE SAMPLING of texts*

of the same period found in other parts of the world. . . . It is, therefore, most likely that the text on which our modern translations rest [i.e. ERV, RSV, "B" and "Aleph" etc.] *is SIMPLY A VERY EARLY EGYPTIAN FORM OF THE TEXT WHOSE NEARNESS TO THE ORIGINAL IS OPEN TO DEBATE.* [Hodges quoted by Dr. David Otis Dr. Fuller, *Which Bible*, pp. 27-28]

B. The Traditional, Received Text is More U- NIFORM Than "B" or "Aleph." Hodges wrote:

The MAJORITY TEXT [as he calls the Received or Traditional Text] *it must be remembered is RELATIVELY UNIFORM IN ITS GENERAL CHARACTER WITH COMPARATIVELY LOW AMOUNTS OF VARIATION BETWEEN ITS MAJOR REPRESENTATIVES. No one has yet explained how a long, slow process spread out over many centuries as well as over a wide geographical area, and involving a multitude of copyists, who often knew nothing of the state of the text outside of their own monasteries or scriptoria, could achieve this WIDESPREAD UNIFORMITY out of the diversity presented by the earlier forms of text. . . Herein lies the greatest weakness of contemporary textual criticism. Denying to the MAJORITY TEXT any claim to represent the actual form of the original text, it is nevertheless UNABLE TO EXPLAIN ITS RISE, ITS COMPARATIVE UNIFORMITY, AND ITS DOMINANCE IN ANY SATISFACTORY MANNER. All these factors can rationally be accounted for, however, if the MAJORITY TEXT represents simply the CONTINUOUS TRANSMISSION OF THE ORIGINAL TEXT FROM THE VERY FIRST. All minority text forms are, on this view* [this would include "B" and "Aleph"], *merely DIVERGENT OFFSHOOTS OF THE BROAD STREAM OF TRANSMISSION WHOSE SOURCE IS THE AUTOGRAPHS THEMSELVES.* [Hodges quoted by Dr. David Otis Dr. Fuller, *Which Bible*, p. 35]

C. Burgon Crushed the Argument of Manuscript Age Used by Followers of "B" and "Aleph." Dean Burgon wrote;

I request that apart from PROOF OF SOME SORT, IT SHALL NOT BE TAKEN FOR GRANTED THAT A COPY OF THE NEW TESTAMENT WRITTEN IN THE FOURTH OR FIFTH CENTURY [like "B" and "Aleph"] *WILL EXHIBIT A MORE TRUSTWORTHY TEXT THAN ONE WRITTEN IN THE 11th OR 12th CENTURY.* [Dean Burgon quoted by Dr. David Otis Dr. Fuller, *Which Bible*, p. 124]

D. Hoskier Put the False Argument of West-

cott and Hort into Proper Perspective. Herman C.

Hoskier wrote:

> *Those who accept the W & H text* [that is, Westcott and Hort Text] *are basing their accusations of untruth as to the Gospellists upon an EGYPTIAN REVISION CURRENT 200 to 450 A.D. AND ABANDONED BETWEEN 500 and 1881, MERELY REVIVED IN OUR DAY AND STAMPED AS GENUINE.* [Hoskier quoted by Dr. David Otis Dr. Fuller, *Which Bible*, p. 263; quoting from Herman Hoskier's *Codex B and Its Allies*, Volume I, pp. 468-469 which is **B.F.T. #1643** @ $46 +S&H).

This is an astute summation of the argument to this point.

E. Even Dr. Hort Admitted the First "Ancestor" of the Received Text Was At Least Contemporary with His "B" and "Aleph". Wilkinson, quoting an-

other, wrote:

> *. . . the first ancestor of the RECEIVED TEXT was, AS DR. HORT IS CAREFUL TO REMIND US, AT LEAST CONTEMPORARY WITH THE OLDEST OF OUR EXTANT MANUSCRIPTS IF NOT OLDER THAN ANY ONE OF THEM."* [Wilkinson quoted by Dr. David Otis Dr. Fuller, *Which Bible*, p. 227]

F.   Evidence and Argument Indicating the King James Translators in 1611 Had Access to the Types of Greek Texts as Found in "A," "B," and "Aleph," but Rejected Them as Corrupted.

Those who favor the Westcott and Hort manuscripts of "B" and "Aleph" often say that the KJB had no chance to make use of the Greek variations in these manuscripts in 1611. This is false and misleading.

1. Sources were About the Same in 390, 1590 or 1890 A.D. So Far as Varieties of Greek Text is Concerned. Wilkinson quoted Doctor Jacobus on

this:

> *On the whole, the differences in the matter of the sources available in 390, 1590 and 1890 are not very serious.* [Wilkinson quoting Jacobus quoted by Dr. David Otis Dr. Fuller, *Which Bible*, p. 250]

This is as to VARIETY of the type of texts, not necessarily as to QUANTITY of classified manuscripts on hand.

2. The Possibility that the KJB Translators Had Access to Alexandrinus or "A."

Wilkinson wrote:

a. Manuscript "A" or Alexandrin-

us, Arrived in London in 1627. Though it was true that "The Alexandrinus Manuscript ["A"] arrived in London in 1627" [Dr. David Otis Dr. Fuller, *Which Bible*, p. 251], what was to prevent the King James Translators from having access to it while in the possession of its owner, Cyril Lucar (1568-1638), who, in "1602" was "elected Patriarch of Alexandria, Egypt, where the Alexandrinus Manuscript had been kept for years?" [Dr. David Otis Dr. Fuller, *Which Bible*, p. 251] As the "Head of the Greek Catholic Church," [Dr. David Otis Dr. Fuller, *Which Bible, loc. cit.*] he was known to be friendly to and a "great admirer of the Protestant Reformation" as well as "an earnest opponent of Rome." [Wilkinson quoted by Dr. David Otis Dr. Fuller, *Which Bible*, p. 252]

b. Summary of Argument for Access to "A" by the KJB Translators. Wilkinson wrote:

We think enough has been given to show that the scholars of Europe and England, in particular, had ample opportunity to BECOME FULLY ACQUAINTED by 1611 with the PROBLEMS INVOLVED IN THE ALEXANDRINUS MANUSCRIPT [or "A"]. [Wilkinson quoted by Dr. David Otis Dr. Fuller, *Which Bible*, p. 252]

3. The Possibility that the KJB Translators had Access to Vaticanus or "B." Wilkinson pointed out a few facts on this matter:

a. The Old Testament Vaticanus was Printed Since 1587.

We are told that the Old Testament portion of the Vaticanus ["B"] has been printed since 1587.

The third great edition is that commonly known as the "Sixtine," published at Rome in 1587 under Pope Sixtus V. . . . Substantially, the "Sixtine" edition gives the text of B [or Vaticanus]*. . . The "Sixtine" served as the basis for most of the ordinary editions of the LXX for just three centuries."* [Wilkinson quoted by Dr. David Otis Dr. Fuller, *Which Bible*, p. 255]

b. Erasmus Could Have Had Access to the Old Testament "B" or Could Have Had a Copy of the O.T. "B." Wilkinson wrote:

We are informed by another author that, if ERASMUS had desired, he could have secured a transcript of this manuscript. [That is, an O.T. "B"] *There was no necessity, however, for ERASMUS to obtain a transcript because he was in correspondence with Professor Paulus Bombasius at Rome, who SENT HIM SUCH VARIANT READINGS AS HE WISHED.* [Wilkinson quoted by Dr. David Otis Dr. Fuller, *Which Bible*, p, 253]

c. Erasmus Found the Received Text to be Superior to the Vaticanus, or "B."

Will-chanson wrote:

> *A correspondent of Erasmus in 1533 sent that scholar a number of selected readings from it* [Codex B], *as proof of its superiority to the RECEIVED GREEK TEXT. ERASMUS, however, REJECTED THESE VARYING READINGS OF THE VATICAN MANUSCRIPT* ["B"] *BECAUSE HE CONSIDERED FROM THE MASSIVE EVIDENCE OF HIS DAY THAT THE RECEIVED TEXT WAS CORRECT.* [Wilkinson quoted by Dr. David Otis Dr. Fuller, *Which Bible*, p. 253]

4. The Possibility that the KJB Translators Had Access to Sinaiticus or "Aleph," or Texts of the Same General Type.

a. How Tischendorf Found Sinaiticus or "Aleph" in 1844. Wilkinson observed:

> *Tischendorf was visiting this monastery* [that is, at the foot of Mt. Sinai] *in 1844 to look for these documents. He discovered IN A BASKET over forty pages of a Greek manuscript of the Bible. He was told that two other basket loads had been USED FOR KINDLING. Later, in 1859, he again visited this monastery to search for other manuscripts. He was about to give up in despair and depart when he was told of a bundle of additional leaves of a Greek manuscript. When he examined the contents of this bundle, he saw them to be a reproduction of part of the Bible in Greek.* [Wilkinson quoted by Dr. David Otis Dr. Fuller, *Which Bible*, p. 254]

b. The Sinaitic "Aleph" is Similar to the Vaticanus "B" in Text. Wilkinson wrote:

> *We have already given authorities to show that the SINAITIC MANUSCRIPT* ["Aleph"] *is a brother of the VATICANUS* ["B"]. *Therefore, THE TRANSLATORS OF 1611 HAD AVAILABLE ALL THE VARIANT READINGS OF THESE MANUSCRIPTS AND REJECTED THEM.* [Wilkinson quoted by Dr. David Otis Dr. Fuller, *Which Bible*, p. 254]

c. Dr. Kendrick, Catholic Bishop of Philadelphia, Confirms that the KJB Translators Knew the Readings of "Aleph" and Other Such Manuscripts. Wilkinson stated:

> *The following words from Dr. Kendrick, Catholic Bishop of*

Philadelphia, will support the conclusion that the translators of the King James KNEW THE READINGS OF CODICES ALEPH, A, B, C, D, where they differed from the RECEIVED TEXT and DENOUNCED THEM. Bishop Kenrick published an English translation of the Catholic Bible in 1849. I quote from the preface:

> *"Since the famous manuscripts of Rome, Alexandria, Cambridge, Paris, and Dublin, were examined . . . a verdict has been obtained in favor of the Vulgate.*

> *"At the Reformation, the Greek Text, as it then stood, was taken as a STANDARD, IN CONFORMITY TO WHICH THE VERSIONS OF THE REFORMERS WERE GENERALLY MADE; whilst the LATIN VULGATE WAS DEPRECIATED, OR DESPISED, as a mere version."*

In other words, the readings of these much boasted manuscripts [that is, "Aleph" and "B"] recently made available, ARE THOSE OF THE VULGATE. The Reformers knew of these readings and REJECTED THEM, AS WELL AS THE VULGATE. [Wilkinson quoted by Dr. David Otis Dr. Fuller, *Which Bible*, pp. 254-255]

This is an important link in the chain of evidence and argument.

G. Even if the KJB Translators Didn't Have "A" "B," and "Aleph" Directly, the Cursives Gave Them All the Variations of These Manuscripts and They Still Rejected Their Readings.

Wilkinson explained:

1. The Difference Between Uncials and Cursives.

> *Just a word on the TWO STYLES OF MANUSCRIPTS before we go further. Manuscripts are of TWO KINDS --UNCIAL AND CURSIVE. UNCIALS are written in large square letters much like our capital letters; CURSIVES are of a free running hand.* [Wilkinson quoted by Dr. David Otis Dr. Fuller, *Which Bible*, p, 254] [See above, Chapter II, II, for numbers of UNCIALS and CURSIVES in existence today]

2. The KJB Translators Definitely Had Access to Cursives Which Had the Same Prob- lems as "Aleph" and "B." Wilkinson wrote:

> *Let us suppose, for the sake of argument, that the translators of 1611 did NOT have access to the problems of the Alexandrinus, ["A"] the Sinaiticus, ["Aleph"] and Vaticanus ["B"] by DIRECT CONTACT with these UNCIALS. It mattered little. They had OTHER MANU-SCRIPTS [that is, cursives] accessible which PRESENTED ALL THE SAME PROBLEMS.* [Wilkinson quoted by Dr. David Otis Dr. Fuller,

Which Bible, p. 255].

 It is then clear that among the cursive and uncial manuscripts which the Reformers possessed, the MAJORITY agreed with the RECEIVED TEXT; however, there were a few among these documents which belonged to the COUNTERFEIT FAMILY [that is, the family of "B" and "Aleph"]. *These dissenting FEW presented ALL THE PROBLEMS WHICH CAN BE FOUND IN THE ALEXANDRINUS* ["A"], *the VATICANUS* ["B"], *and the SINAITICUS* ["Aleph"]. *In other words, the translators of the KING JAMES came to a DIAMETRICALLY OPPOSITE CONCLUSION FROM THAT ARRIVED AT BY THE REVISERS OF 1881, ALTHOUGH THE MEN OF 1611, AS WELL AS THOSE OF 1881, HAD BEFORE THEM THE SAME PROBLEMS AND THE SAME EVIDENCE.* [Wilkinson quoted by Dr. David Otis Dr. Fuller, *Which Bible*, pp. 255-256]

This is an important point to grasp firmly. It is a favorite, though false, argument of the "B" and "Aleph" devotees.

3. Cursive Copies are Important in Sound Textual Criticism Since They Exhibit All the Phenomena of the Uncials. Wilkinson quoted Dean Burgon and Miller on this point:

 The popular notion seems to be that we are indebted for our knowledge of the TRUE TEXTS of Scripture to the existing UNCIALS ENTIRELY; and that the essence of the secret dwells EXCLUSIVELY WITH THE FOUR OR FIVE OLDEST OF THESE UNCIALS ["B" and "Aleph," A, C, and D, and a few others]. *By consequence, it is popularly supposed that since we are possessed of such UNCIAL copies, WE COULD AFFORD TO DISPENSE WITH THE TESTIMONY OF THE CURSIVES ALTOGETHER. A more complete MISCONCEPTION OF THE FACTS OF THE CASE CAN HARDLY BE IMAGINED. For the plain truth is that ALL THE PHENOMENA EXHIBITED BY THE UNCIAL MANUSCRIPTS ARE REPRODUCED BY THE CURSIVE COPIES."* [Wilkinson quoted by Dr. David Otis Dr. Fuller, *Which Bible*, p. 256]

4. The Cursives are Careful Transmis- sions of the Traditional, Received Text. Wilkinson quoted H. C. Hoskier on this:

 Our experience among the GREEK CURSIVES proves to us that TRANSMISSION HAS NOT BEEN CARELESS, AND THEY DO REPRESENT A WHOLESOME TRADITIONAL TEXT in the passages involving doctrine and so forth. [Wilkinson quoted by Dr. David Otis Dr. Fuller, *Which Bible*, p. 256]

5. The Revisers of the ERV of 1881 Ig- nored All Manuscripts Except About Three or Four. Wilkinson wrote:

On the other hand, if more manuscripts have been made accessible since 1611, LITTLE USE HAS BEEN MADE OF WHAT WE HAD BEFORE AND OF THE MAJORITY OF THOSE MADE AVAILABLE SINCE. The REVISERS SYSTEMATICALLY IGNORED THE WHOLE WORLD OF MANUSCRIPTS AND RELIED PRACTICALLY ON ONLY THREE OR FOUR. As Dean Burgon says,

"But NINETEEN-TWENTIETHS [that is, 95%] of those documents, for any use which has been made of them [by the ERV translators and by Westcott and Hort, that is] might just as well be still LYING IN THE MONASTIC LIBRARIES FROM WHICH THEY WERE OBTAINED."

We feel, therefore, that a mistaken picture of the case has been presented with reference to the MATERIAL AT THE DISPOSITION OF THE TRANSLATORS OF 1611 AND CONCERNING THEIR ABILITY TO USE THAT MATERIAL. [Wilkinson quoted by Dr. David Otis Dr. Fuller, *Which Bible*, pp. 256-257; quoting Dean John William Burgon, in *The Traditional Text*, p. xii which is **B.F.T. #1159** @$16+S&H.]

H. Dr. Hort Admitted that the Cursives Were Almost Identical, but Still Rejected Their Witness in Favor of the False "B" and "Aleph." Wilkinson stat- ed, quoting Hort:

While of the Greek New Testament, DR. HORT, WHO WAS AN OPPONENT OF THE RECEIVED TEXT and who dominated the English New Testament Revision Committee, says, "An OVER-WHELMING PROPORTION OF THE TEXT IN ALL KNOWN CURSIVE MANUSCRIPTS EXCEPT A FEW IS, AS A MATTER OF FACT, IDENTICAL." [Wilkinson quoted by Dr. David Otis Dr. Fuller, *Which Bible*, p. 264]

I. Dr. Hort's Prejudice Against the Received Text Since the Age of 23. Wilkinson wrote:

On what meat had DR. HORT fed, when he dared, being ONLY TWENTY-THREE YEARS OLD, to call the RECEIVED TEXT "villainous" and "vile"? By his own confession, he had at that time READ LITTLE OF THE GREEK-NEW TESTAMENT, AND KNEW NOTHING OF TEXTS AND CERTAINLY NOTHING OF HEBREW. [Wilkinson quoted by Dr. David Otis Dr. Fuller, *Which Bible*, p. 302]

CHAPTER VI
CORRUPTION IN THE "B" AND "ALEPH" MANUSCRIPTS

I. "B" And "Aleph's" Corruption in General

A. A Chronology of Attempts to Corrupt the Traditional Text. As has already been quoted in Chapter III, I, A, in this study, the following is a chronology of how the original manuscripts of the Bible got corrupted, and when. Hills postulated:

1. **Apostolic Age (33-100 A.D.)** The original text was written by the Apostles.

2. **Early Church Period (100-312 A.D.)** The original text was CORRUPTED BY ALEXANDRIAN AND WESTERN SCRIBES. The beginning of the Western Text and the Alexandrian Text.

3. **Byzantine Period (312-1453 A.D.)** The original text was RECOVERED IN THE 4TH CENTURY AND USED BY THE GREEK CHURCH FOR 1,000 YEARS.

4. **Early Modern Period (1453-1831 A.D.)** The original text was printed with slight alterations in 1516. USED BY ALL PROTESTANTS. SOURCE OF THE KING JAMES BIBLE. [Dr. Edward F. Hills, *Believing Bible Study*, p. 184 (1967)]

B. The Antiquity of "B" or "Aleph" Provides No Security That It Was Not CORRUPTED By Heretics At An Early Age. Dean John W. Burgon, as quoted by Dr. Fuller, wrote:

Therefore, [Burgon said] *antiquity alone affords NO SECURITY THAT THE MANUSCRIPT IN OUR HANDS IS NOT INFECTED WITH THE CORRUPTION WHICH SPRANG UP LARGELY IN THE FIRST AND SECOND CENTURIES."* [Dr. David Otis Dr. Fuller, *Which Bible*, p. 125; quoting Dean John William Burgon, in *The Traditional Text*, p. 40 which is **B.F.T.** #1159 @$16+S&H.]

C. "B" and "Aleph" Contain False Readings Due to Deliberate Falsification and to Efforts to "Improve the New Testament Text." Hills quoted Dean

Burgon's views on this subject:

Burgon attributed the FALSE READINGS present in B, Aleph, D, and the other non-Byzantine manuscripts to TWO PRINCIPAL CAUSES. THE FIRST OF THESE WAS THE DELIBERATE FALSIFICATION OF THE NEW TESTAMENT SCRIPTURES BY HERETICS DURING THE SECOND AND THIRD CENTURIES. The SECOND was the doubtless well meant but nevertheless DISASTROUS EFFORTS OF CERTAIN LEARNED CHRISTIANS DURING THIS SAME EARLY PERIOD TO IMPROVE THE NEW TESTAMENT TEXT THROUGH THE USE OF "CONJECTURAL EMENDATION." In support of these contentions Burgon brought forth a number of quotations from the writings of the Church Fathers. [Hills quoted by Dr. David Otis Dr. Fuller, *Which Bible*, pp. 94-95]

This same sort of "CONJECTURAL EMENDATION" is used in the Hebrew edition of the American Bible Society edited by Kittel called the *Biblia Hebraica* and the Stuttgart edition of *Biblia Hebraica* as well. Both of these false Hebrew Texts have been used in the Hebrew departments even of so-called "conservative" theological seminaries in our country.

D. Burgon Charged "B" and "Aleph" with Being Products of "SEMI-ARIAN" Opinions. Dean

Burgon wrote:

The fact is that B and Aleph were THE PRODUCTS OF THE SCHOOL OF PHILOSOPHY and teaching which found its vent in SEMI-ARIAN or HOMOEAN OPINIONS. It is a circumstance that cannot fail to give rise to suspicion that the VATICAN ["B"] *and SINAITIC* ["Aleph"] *manuscripts (B and Aleph) had their origin under a PREDOMINANT INFLUENCE OF SUCH EVIL FAME."* [Dr. David Otis Dr. Fuller, *Which Bible*, p. 130; quoting Dean John William Burgon, in *The Traditional Text*, pp. 160-161 which is **B.F.T.** #1159 @$16+S&H.]

E. Hoskier Believed "B" and "Aleph" Contained the False Textual Criticism and Spec-

ulative Philosophies of Origen. Hoskier stated:

The claim of W & H [Westcott and Hort] to have RESURRECTED THE TEXTS of ORIGEN certainly holds good except in certain places. But in doing so they far exceed Origen's own claim. Origen's citations are FULL OF CONFLATIONS, where he knew two recensions and INCORPORATED BOTH. If he was not able to judge which of these was the original, why should he be a perfect judge of other DOUBLE READINGS similarly situated but of which he chose one? . . . And it is not disputed that Origen bestowed special pains upon every department of Biblical criticism and exegesis. His "Hexapla" is a monument of stupendous industry and keen discernment; but his labors on the Old Testament were thwarted by his very imperfect knowledge of Hebrew, and BY THE TENDENCY TO MYSTIC INTERPRETATIONS COMMON IN HIS OWN LAN-GUAGE, BUT IN NO OTHER WRITER SO FULLY DEVELOPED OR PUSHED TO THE SAME EXTREMES. [Hoskier quoted by Dr. David Otis Dr. Fuller, *Which Bible*, pp. 139-140]

For a comparison of Origen's more well-known heresies and strange, twisted and perverted views of the Scriptural doctrines and methods, see *A History Of Christian Thought: Volume One:* "History of Christian Doctrine" by Dr. J. L. Neve, Philadelphia, The Muhlenberg Press, 1946, 344 pages. See pages 13, 79, 83ff., 108, 112, 114, 119, 139, 154, 160, 166, 167, 169, 186, 220, 249, 261, 270.

F. At Least 80 Heretical Parties Were Prevalent in the Early Church to Corrupt the Manu- scripts. Wilkinson wrote:

HERETICAL SECTS, warring for supremacy, CORRUPTED THE MANUSCRIPTS IN ORDER TO FURTHER THEIR ENDS. "Epiphanius, in his polemic treatise the 'Panarion,' describes not less than EIGHTY HERETICAL PARTIES." [Wilkinson quoting Fisher's History of Christian Doctrine, p. 19]; [Dr. David Otis Dr. Fuller, *Which Bible*, p. 182]

G. Wilkinson Named Four Men as being the Leaders in Corrupting "B" and "Aleph." He wrote:

Beginning shortly after the death of the apostle John, FOUR NAMES STAND OUT IN PROMINENCE whose teachings CONTRIBUTED BOTH TO THE VICTORIOUS HERESY AND TO THE FINAL ISSUING OF MANUSCRIPTS OF A CORRUPT NEW TESTAMENT [such as in "B" and "Aleph"]. *These names are (1) JUSTIN MARTYR, (2) TATIAN, (3) CLEMENT OF ALEXANDRIA, and (4) ORIGEN.* [Wilkinson quoted by Dr. David Otis Dr. Fuller, *Which Bible*, p. 181]

Wilkinson then traces just how each of these four HERETICS contributed to the

CORRUPTING of the Greek texts.

H. The Heresy of Gnosticism was a Cause of Corruption in Some Texts Also. Hills wrote:

Traces of GNOSTICISM seem clearly discernible in Papyrus Bodmer III, a Bohairic manuscript which was published in 1958. . . E. Massaux (1959) points out the following instances of the FALSE INTELLECTUALISM WHICH CHARACTERIZED THE GNOSTICS, namely their preoccupation with the notion of TRUTH and the substitution of TRUTH for RIGHTEOUSNESS. [Dr. Edward F. Hills, *Believing Bible Study*, p. 135 (1967)]

II. Specific Examples of Textual Corruption in the "B" and "Aleph" Family of Alexandrian Manuscripts in Matters of Doctrinal Importance.

A. Some of the Editions of the Bible Which Have Followed "B" and "Aleph" in Their Doctrinal Corruptions. Jasper James Ray, in his book, *God Wrote Only One Bible*, laid out some of the versions in history which have followed "B" and "Aleph" all of which are forerunners of the ERV of 1881; the ASV of 1901, and the RSV of 1952. He listed: (1) Sinaiticus, 331 A.D.; (2) Vaticanus, 331 A.D.; (3) Jerome's Vulgate, 382 A.D.; (4) Alexandrian, 450 A.D.; (5) Ephraem, 450 A.D.; (6) Douay, 1582 A.D.; (7) Clementine Vulgate, 1592 A.D.; (8) Griesbach, 1805 A.D.; (9) Lachmann, 1850 A.D.; (10) Wordsworth, 1870 A.D.; (11) Tregelles, 1870 A.D.; (12) Tischendorf, 1872; (13) Alford, 1872 A.D.; (14) Westcott and Hort, 1881; (15) All others departing from the *Textus Receptus*; (16) English Revised Version, 1881; (17) Nestle's 1898; (18) American Standard Version, 1901; (19) Revised Standard Version of the NCC, 1952. [Jasper James Ray, *God Wrote Only One Bible*, p. 71]

B. Some of the Editions of the Bible Which Have Followed the Original *Textus Receptus* for the Most Part, and Which Do Not Have These Specific Doctrinal Corruptions. Ray listed the following: (1) Peshitta Bible,, 150 A.D.; (2) Itala Bible, 157 A.D.; (3) Erasmus Bible, 1522 A.D.; (4) Tyndale's Bible, 1525; (5) Luther's Bible, 1534; (6) Coverdale Bible, 1535 A.D.; (7) Matthew's Bible, 1537 A.D.; (8) The Great Bible, 1539 A.D.; (9) Stephen's Bible, 1550 A.D.; (10) Geneva Bible, 1560 A.D.; (11) Bishop's Bible,

1568 A.D.; (12) Beza's Bible, 1604 A.D.; (13) KING JAMES BIBLE, 1611. [Jasper James Ray, *God Wrote Only One Bible*, p. 109]

C. The Plan of Ray's Work.

1. The 44 Bible Versions or Translations Tested by Ray in Order of Bad to Good, from the Standpoint of Using the Received Text in the Verses in Question.

Ray, in his book, examined the following 44 versions or translations and checked them as to whether or not they followed "B" and "Aleph" or the Westcott and Hort Greek Text with respect to 162 key verses. I have included the percentage of times in the 162 verses that the translation in question follows the corrupt "B" and "Aleph" readings and rejected the Traditional, Received text of the KJB in the Greek.

Greek Text or English Translation	Verses out of Possible 162 Where Parts of the Verse Omitted	Percentage of Parts of Verses Omitted
1. Revised Standard Version	158/162	98%
2. Nestle's Greek Text	155/162	96%
3. Goodspeed's New Testament	54/162	95%
4. Westcott & Hort's Greek Text	151/162	93%
5. Tischendorf's Greek N.T.	150/162	92%
6. New English New Testament	150/162	92%
7. Williams' New Testament	149/126	92%
8. Berkeley Version N.T.	148/162	92%
9. New American Standard	147/162	91%
10. Riverside New Testament	147/162	91%
11. New World Translation	145/162	89%
12. Good News for Modern Man (TEV)	144/162	89%
13. Moffatt's New Testament	144/162	89%
14. Von Soden's New Testament	143/162	88%
15. Wuest's Expanded N.T.	142/162	88%
16. Twentieth Century N.T.	142/162	88%
17. Tregelles' Greek N.T.	140/162	86%
18. Weymouth's New Testament	138/162	85%
19. Panin's Numeric N.T.	138/162	85%
20. Moulton's New Testament	137/162	85%
21. Amplified New Testament	136/162	84%
22. Alford's Greek N.T.	134/162	83%
23. Revised Version of 1881	135/162	84%
24. American Standard Version of 1901	135/162	84%

25. Godbey's New Testament	132/162	81%
26. Parallel Column N.T.	131/162	81%
27. Diaglot New Testament	128/162	79%
28. Montgomery's N.T.	124/162	76%
29. Lachmann's Greek N.T.	121/162	75%
30. Phillip's New Testament	117/162	72%
31. Living N.T. Paraphrased	114/162	70%
32. Ferrer Fenton's N.T.	112/162	69%
33. Latin New Testament	96/162	59%
34. Darby's New Testament	93/162	57%
35, Confraternity N.T.	90/162	55%
36. Douay Version N.T.	75/162	46%
37. Griesbach's Greek N.T.	61/162	38%
38. Wordsworth's Greek N.T.	47/162	29%
39. Norlie's Simplified N.T.	41/162	25%
40. Lamsa's New Testament	40/162	25%
41. John Wesley's N.T.	38/162	23%
42. Martin Luther's German N.T.	0/162	0%
43. *Textus Receptus* Greek N.T.	0/162	0%
44. King James New Testament	0/162	0%

[Jasper James Ray, *God Wrote Only One Bible*, pp. 33-34]

2. The 162 Verses Which Have Parts or the Whole Omitted in the "B" and/or "Aleph" Corruptions (or their English Counterparts) for the Most Part, as Examined by Ray.

Ray listed the following verses which he checked in all of the above 44 versions and/or translations of the New Testament to find out if there were omissions in whole or in part of the verses in question.

1.	Matthew 1:25	14.	Matthew 1:16
2.	Matthew 6:33	15.	Matthew 20:7
3.	Matthew 8:29	16.	Matthew 20:16
4.	Matthew 9:13	17.	Matthew 20:22
5.	Matthew 12:35	18.	Matthew 23:14
6.	Matthew 12:47	19.	Matthew 25:13
7.	Matthew 13:51	20.	Matthew 27:35
8.	Matthew 16:3	21.	Matthew 28:2
9.	Matthew 16:20	22.	Matthew 28:9
10.	Matthew 18:11	23.	Mark 1:1
11.	Matthew 19:9	24.	Mark 1:14
12.	Matthew 19:17	25.	Mark 2:17
13.	Matthew 17:21	26.	Mark 6:11

27.	Mark 7:16	70.	John 11:41
28.	Mark 9:24	71.	John 16:16
29.	Mark 9:42	72.	John 17:12
30.	Mark 9:44,46	73.	John 20:29
31.	Mark 10:21	74.	Acts 2:30
32.	Mark 11:10	75.	Acts 7:30
33.	Mark 11:26	76.	Acts 7:37
34.	Mark 12:29-30	77.	Acts 8:37
35.	Mark 13:14	78.	Acts 9:5-6
36.	Mark 14:68	79.	Acts 10:6
37.	Mark 15:28	80.	Acts 16:31
38.	Mark 16:9-20	81.	Acts 17:26
39.	Luke 1:28,	82.	Acts 20:25
40.	Luke 2:33	83.	Acts 20:32
41.	Luke 2:43	84.	Acts 23:9
42.	Luke 4:4	85.	Acts 24:6-8
43.	Luke 4:8	86.	Acts 24:15
44.	Luke 4:41	87.	Acts 28:16
45.	Luke 7:31	88.	Acts 28:29
46.	Luke 9:54	89.	Romans 1:16
47.	Luke 11;29	90.	Romans 5:2
48.	Luke 22;31	91.	Romans 9:28
49.	Luke 23:17	92.	Romans 11:6
50.	Luke 23:38	93.	Romans 13:9
51.	Luke 23:42	94.	Romans 14:6
52.	Luke 24:12	95.	Romans 14:9
53.	Luke-24:40	96.	Romans 14:21
54.	Luke 24:49	97.	Romans 15:29
55.	Luke 24:51	98.	Romans 16:24
56,	John 1:14	99.	1 Corinthians 1:14
57.	John 1:18	100	1 Corinthians 5:7
58.	John 1:27	101	1 Corinthians 6:20
59.	John 3:13	102	1 Corinthians 7:39
60.	John 3:15	103	1 Corinthians 10:28
61.	John 3:16	104	1 Corinthians 11:24
62.	John 3:18	105	1 Corinthians 11;29
63.	John 4:42	106	1 Corinthians 15:47
64.	John 5:3	107	1 Corinthians 16:22
65.	John 5:4	108	1 Corinthians 16:23
66.	John 6:47	109	2 Corinthians 4:6
67.	John 7:53-8:11	110	2 Corinthians 4:10
68.	John 8:16	111.	Galatians 3:1
69.	John 9:35	112.	Galatians 4:7

113. Galatians 6:15
114. Ephesians 3:9
115. Ephesians 3:14
116. Philippians 3:16
117. Colossians 1:2
118. Colossians 1:14
119. 1 Thessalonians 1:1
120. 1 Thessalonians 3:11
121. 2 Thessalonians 1:8
122. 1 Timothy 3:16
123. 1 Timothy 6:5
124. 2 Timothy 1:11
125. 2 Timothy 4:22
126. Titus 1:4
127. Hebrews 1:3
128. Hebrews 2:7
129. Hebrews 2:11
130. Hebrews 7:21
131. Hebrews 10:30
132. Hebrews 10:34
133. Hebrews 11:11
134, James 5:16
135. 1 Peter 1;22
136. 1 Peter 4;1
137. 1 Peter 4:14
138. 1 Peter 5:10
139. 1 Peter 5:11

140. 2 Peter 2:17
141. 1 John 1:7
142. 1 John 2:7
143. 1 John 4:3
144. 1 John 4:9
145. 1 John 4:19
146. 1 John 5:7-8
147. Jude 25
148. Revelation 1:8
149. Revelation 1:9
150. Revelation 1:11
151. Revelation 2:13
152. Revelation 5:14
153. Revelation 6:1,3,5,7
154. Revelation 11:17
155. Revelation 12:12
156. Revelation 12:17
157. Revelation 14:5
158. Revelation 16:3,8,10,12,17
159. Revelation 16:17
160. Revelation 20:9
161. Revelation 20:12
162. Revelation 21:24
      [Jasper James Ray, *God Wrote Only One Bible*, pp. 36-55]

D. Specific Examples of Corruption of the Text of "B" and "Aleph" (or their English Count- erparts) for the Most Part Involving Doctrinal Changes or Omissions.

Bearing in mind the warnings found in 2 John 1:9-11, concerning anyone bringing not "the doctrine of Christ," the following doctrinal topics have been tampered with by change or omission in most of the versions or translations listed under Chapter VI, II, C, 1, above. This has been due to the influence of the "B" and "Aleph" manuscripts or their Alexandrian allies. Not all 162 verses above have been classified by this writer because they do not all involve doctrinal matters as such. I think, however, that the changes which have been made by the falsifying, heretics who tampered with the "B" and "Aleph" family of Greek texts to further their false doctrines, do fit in with the false teachings of (1) those who believed in "conjectural emen- dation"; (2) Semi-Arianism; (3) Justin Martyr; (4) Tatian; (5) Clement of

Alexandria; (6) Origen; (7) Gnosticism; (8) Docetism, and some of the other heresies of the 2nd, 3d, and 4th centuries.

1. Omissions Involving the Deity of Christ by Omitting the Word "Lord," and in Other Ways.

(1) Titus 1:4 ". . . peace from God the Father and [THE LORD] Jesus Christ our Saviour." ["THE LORD" has been omitted in the "B" and "Aleph" texts].

(2) Matthew 8:29. "And, behold, they cried out, saying, What have we to do with thee, Jesus, thou Son [OF GOD]? art thou come hither to torment us before the time?" [BRACKETS INDICATE THE WORDS OMITTED FROM THE VERSE,]

(3) Matthew 19:17. ". . . Why callest thou me good? There is none, good but one, that is, [GOD]; but if thou wilt enter into life, . ."

(4) Mark 1:1. "The beginning of the gospel of Jesus Christ, [THE SON OF GOD]."

(5) Mark 9:24. "the father of the child cried out, and said, with tears, [LORD] I believe, help thou mine unbelief."

(6) Mark 11:10. "Blessed be the kingdom of our father David that cometh [IN THE NAME OF THE LORD]; Hosanna in the highest."

(7) Luke 7.31. "[AND THE LORD SAID] Whereunto then shall I liken the men of this generation?"

(8) Luke 22:31. "[AND THE LORD SAID], Simon, Simon, behold Satan hath desired to have you. . . ."

(9) Luke 23:42. "And he said unto Jesus, [LORD), remember me when thou comest into thy kingdom."

(10) John 9:35. "Dost thou believe on the Son of God? [Changed to "SON OF MAN"]

(11) Acts 8:37. "[AND PHILIP SAID, IF THOU BELIEVEST WITH ALL THINE HEART, THOU MAYEST. AND HE ANSWERED AND SAID, I BELIEVE THAT JESUS CHRIST IS THE SON OF GOD."] [The whole verse is omitted.]

(12) Acts 9:5-6. "1 am Jesus whom thou persecutest: [IT IS HARD FOR THEE TO KICK AGAINST THE PRICKS. AND HE TREMBLING AND ASTONISHED SAID, LORD, WHAT WILT THOU HAVE ME TO DO? AND THE LORD SAID UNTO HIM] Arise and go into the city.

(13) 1 Corinthians 11:29. "damnation to himself,

not discerning [THE LORD'S] body."

(14) 1 Corinthians 15:47. "the second man is [THE LORD] from heaven."

(15) 2 Corinthians 4:10. "Always bearing about in the body the dying of [THE LORD] Jesus.

(16) 1 Timothy 3:16. "And without controversy great is the mystery of godliness: [GOD] [Changed to HE or WHO] was manifest in the flesh, justified in the Spirit.

2. Omissions of Christ's Full Title, "The Lord Jesus Christ."

(1) Romans 16:24. "[THE GRACE OF OUR LORD JESUS CHRIST BE WITH YOU ALL. AMEN. [Entire Verse is omitted.]

(2) Ephesians 3:14. "I bow my knees unto the Father [OF OUR LORD JESUS CHRIST]"

(3) Colossians 1:2. "and peace, from God our Father [AND THE LORD JESUS CHRIST]"

(4) 1 Thessalonians 1:1. "and peace, [FROM GOD THE FATHER AND THE LORD JESUS CHRIST.]"

3. Omissions Involving "Jesus" or "Christ" as Titles for the Lord Jesus Christ.

(1) Matthew 16:20. "Then charged he his disciples that they should tell no man that he was [JESUS] the Christ."

(2) Luke 4:41. "And devils also came out of many crying out, and saying, Thou art [CHRIST] the Son of God. . .

(3) John 4:42. "that this is indeed [THE CHRIST] the Saviour of the world."

(4) Acts 16:31. "Believe on the Lord Jesus [CHRIST] and thou shalt be saved, and thy house,"

(5) 1 Corinthians 16:22. "If any man love not the Lord [JESUS CHRIST], let him be Anathema Maranatha."

(6) 1 Corinthians 16:23. "The grace of our Lord Jesus [CHRIST] be with you."

(7) 2 Corinthians 4:6. "to give the light of the knowledge of the glory of God In the face of [JESUS] Christ."

(8) 1 Thessalonians 3:11. "Now God himself and our Father, and our Lord Jesus [CHRIST] direct our way unto you"

(9) 2 Thessalonians 1:8. "that know not God, and that obey not the gospel of our Lord Jesus [CHRIST]."

(10) 1 Timothy 4:22. "The Lord [JESUS CHRIST] [or] Jesus [CHRIST], be with thy spirit.

(11) 1 Peter 5:10. "hath called us unto his eternal glory by Christ [JESUS], after that ye have suffered . . . "

(12) 1 John 1:7. "and the blood of Jesus [CHRIST] his Son cleanseth us from all sin."

(13) 1 John 4:3. "And every spirit that confesseth that Jesus [CHRIST IS COME IN THE FLESH] is of God."

(14) Revelation 1:9. ". . . and patience of Jesus [CHRIST], was in the isle that is called Patmos,

(15) Revelation 12:17. "and have the testimony of Jesus [CHRIST]."

The omission of either CHRIST or JESUS from the title, "JESUS CHRIST" is to deny the unity of the titles in one Person, each indicating one of Christ's natures, the human and the divine. Heresies today seek to split the so-called "human Jesus" from the "Christ" of deity. The Christian Science cult is one which does this today. There are and were many others.

4. Changes Involving the Matter of Christ's Virgin Birth, Involving the Relationship of Jesus Christ with His Mother and with Joseph.

(1) Luke 2:33. "And Joseph [changed to "HIS FATHER" which weakens, if not denies, the virgin birth of Christ] and his mother marvelled at those things which were spoken of him."

(2) Luke 2:43. "the child Jesus tarried behind in Jerusalem; and Joseph and his mother [changed to "HIS PARENTS"] knew not of it."

(3) Matthew 1:25. "and knew her not till she had brought forth her [FIRSTBORN] son; and he called his name Jesus." [Another weakening of the miraculous virgin birth.]

5. Omissions of "Begotten' Which Alters Christ's Eternal Sonship and Eternal Gener- ation of the Father.

(1) John 3:16. "For God so loved the world that he gave his only [BEGOTTEN] Son." ["BEGOTTEN" is present in the "B" and "Aleph" Greek texts, but is omitted in many modern English versions and perversions. So throughout this section #5.]

(2) John 3;18. ". . . be hath not believed in the name of the only [BEGOTTEN] son of God."

(3) **John 1:14**. "the glory as of the only [BEGOTTEN] of the Father, full of grace and truth."

(4) **John 1:18**. "No man hath seen God at any time; the only [BEGOTTEN] Son, which is in the bosom of the Father, he hath declared him."

(5) **1 John 4.9**. ". . . because that God sent his only [BEGOTTEN] Son into the world."

6. Omissions of "Alpha and Omega" or "Beginning and the Ending," Referring to Christ's Eternal Generation and Future.

(1) **Revelation 1:8**. "1 am Alpha and Omega, [THE BEGINNING AND THE ENDING], saith the Lord."

(2) **Revelation 1:11**. "Saying, [I AM ALPHA AND OMEGA, THE FIRST AND THE LAST] and What thou seest, write in a book."

7. Omission of Christ's Omnipresence.

John.3:13. ". . . No man hath ascended up to heaven, but he that came down from heaven, even the Son of man [WHICH IS IN HEAVEN]."

8. Omission of Christ's Eternal Future State.

(1) **Revelation 5:14**.   "fell down and worshipped [HIM THAT LIVETH FOR EVER AND EVER.]"

(2) **Revelation 11:17**.   "which art and wast [AND ART TO COME]; because thou hast taken to thee thy great power"

9. Omission of Christ's Part in Creation.

Ephesians 3:9. "Mystery which from the beginning of the world hath been hid in God who created all things [BY JESUS CHRIST]."

10. Omission of the Fact that Salvation is Only Through Jesus Christ and Our Personal Faith in Him.

(1) **Matthew 18:11**. "[FOR THE SON OF MAN IS COME TO SAVE THAT WHICH WAS LOST.]" [The entire verse was omitted.]

(2) **Mark 9:42**. "And whosoever shall offend one of these little ones that believe [IN ME] it is better for him that a millstone . . ."

(3) **John 6:47**. "Verily, verily I say unto you, He that believeth [ON ME] hath everlasting life."

(4) Romans 15:29. 1 shall come in the fulness of the blessing [OF THE GOSPEL] of Christ."

(5) Romans 1:16. "For I am not ashamed of the gospel [OF CHRIST]; for it is the power of God . . ."

(6) 1 Corinthians 5:7. "ye are unleavened. For even Christ our passover is sacrificed [FOR US]."

(7) Galatians 4:7. "but a son; and if a son, then an heir of God [THROUGH CHRIST.]"

(8) Galatians 6:15. "For [IN CHRIST JESUS] neither circumcision availeth anything nor uncircumcision, but a new creature."

(9) Colossians 1:14. "In whom we have redemption [THROUGH HIS BLOOD], even the forgiveness of sins."

(10) Hebrews 1:3. "when he had [BY HIMSELF] purged our sins, sat down on the right hand . . ."

(11) 1 Peter 4:1. "as Christ hath suffered [FOR US] in the flesh . . ."

11. Omissions or Weakening of Christ's Bodily Resurrection.

(1) Romans 14:9. "For to this end Christ [BOTH] died, [AND ROSE], and revived, that he might be Lord both of the dead and living."

(2) Acts 24:15. "that there shall be a resurrection [OF THE DEAD] both of the just and unjust."

(3) Luke 24:12. "[THEN AROSE PETER, AND RAN UNTO THE SEPULCHRE, AND STOOPING DOWN, HE BEHELD THE LINEN CLOTHES LAID BY THEMSELVES, AND DEPARTED, WONDERING IN HIMSELF AT THAT WHICH WAS COME TO PASS."] [The entire verse is omitted by some Greek manuscripts.]

(4) Luke 24:40. ["AND WHEN HE HAD THUS SPOKEN, HE SHOWED THEM HIS HANDS AND HIS FEET."] [The entire verse is omitted by some Greek manuscripts.] Psalms says that they pierced His "feet" and this is the only New Testament reference. Hills described the heresies of Marcion and the DOCETISTS who denied Christ came in the flesh (1 John 4:3); denied Christ's body was a true body, hence Luke 24:39 and 40. [Dr. Edward F. Hills, *Believing Bible Study*, pp. 129-130 (1967)]

(5) Acts 2:30. ". . . that of the fruit of his loins, [ACCORDING TO THE FLESH HE WOULD RAISE UP CHRIST] to sit on his throne."

12. Omission of Christ's Bodily Ascen-

sion.

(1) **Luke 24:51**. "And it came to pass, while he blessed them, he was parted from them [AND CARRIED UP INTO HEAVEN.]"

(2) **John 16:16**. "and ye shall see me [BECAUSE I GO TO THE FATHER.]"

13. Omission of Christ's Bodily Return.

Matthew 25:13. "Watch therefore, for ye know neither the day nor the hour [WHEREIN THE SON OF MAN COMETH."]

14. Omission of Christ's Great Commision.

Mark 16:15. ["GO YE INTO ALL THE WORLD AND PREACH THE GOSPEL TO EVERY CREATURE."] [This is omitted from both "B" and "Aleph."]

15. Omission of the Woman Taken in Adultery.

John 7:53--8:11. [Entire story of the woman taken in adultery is omitted, all 12 verses of it.] Dean Burgon defended this passage by saying:

I contend that on all intelligent principles of sound criticism the passage before us [that is, John 7:53-8:11] must be maintained to be genuine scripture and that without a particle of doubt. Burgon requests the student to go to the British museum and ask for the 73 copies of John's Gospel, turn to the close of chapter 7 and in 61 copies [or 84% of them] You will find these verses 8:1-11. [Dr. David Otis Dr. Fuller, *Which Bible*, pp. 123-124]

For Dean Burgon's full treatment on these verses, consult his book, *The Last Twelve Verses of Mark* which is **B.F.T. #1139** perfect bound @ **$15.00 +S&H**.

16. Omission or Weakening of Eternal Punishment in Hell and Other Judgment.

(1) **Mark 9:44, 46**. "[WHERE THEIR WORM DIETH NOT AND THE FIRE IS NOT QUENCHED] . . . [WHERE THEIR WORM DIETH NOT AND THE FIRE IS NOT QUENCHED.] [Omitted in both verses.]

(2) **2 Peter 2:17**. "to whom the mist of darkness is reserved [FOR EVER]."

(3) **Mark 6:11**. "shake off the dust under your feet for a testimony against them, [VERILY I SAY UNTO YOU, IT SHALL BE MORE TOLERABLE FOR SODOM AND GOMORRAH IN THE DAY OF JUDGMENT THAN FOR THAT CITY.]"

(4) John 3:15, "That whosoever believeth in him [SHOULD NOT PERISH BUT] have eternal life."

17. Omission or Downgrading of Heaven.

(1) Hebrews 10:34. "knowing in yourselves that ye have [IN HEAVEN] a better and enduring substance,"

(2) 1 John 5:7-8. "For there are three that bear record [IN HEAVEN, THE FATHER, THE WORD AND THE HOLY GHOST; AND THESE THREE ARE ONE, AND THERE ARE THREE THAT BEAR WITNESS ON EARTH], the Spirit, and the water, and the blood. . . ."

(3) Revelation 16:17. "came a great voice out of the temple [OF HEAVEN] from the throne, saying . . ."

18. Omission or Weakening of Repentance.

(1) Mark 2:17. ". . .I came not to call the righteous, but sinners [TO REPENTANCE]."

(2) Matthew 9:13. "I am not come to call the righteous, but sinners [TO REPENTANCE.]"

19. Omission or Weakening of Salvation by Faith.

Romans 5:2. "By whom also we have access [BY FAITH] into this grace wherein we stand . . ."

20. Omission or Downgrading of the Word of God.

(1) Luke 4:4. ". . . It is written, That man shall not live by bread alone, [BUT BY EVERY WORD OF GOD.]"

(2) Hebrews 10:30. "I will recompense, [SAITH THE LORD], and again. . ."

21. Omission of Phrases that Indicate Fulfilled Old Testament Prophecy.

(1) Luke 11:29. "there shall no sign be given it, but the sign of Jonas [THE PROPHET]."

(2) Luke 9:54. "wilt thou that we command fire to come down from heaven, and consume them [EVEN AS ELIJAH DID?]"

(3) Mark 15:28. "[AND THE SCRIPTURE WAS FULFILLED WHICH SAITH, AND HE WAS NUMBERED WITH THE TRANSGRESSORS."] [All of this is omitted.]

(4) Mark 13:14. "But when ye shall see the

abomination of desolation [SPOKEN OF BY DANIEL THE PROPHET] standing where it ought not. . ."

(5) Matthew 27:35. "And they crucified him, and parted his garments, casting lots; [THAT IT MIGHT BE FULFILLED WHICH WAS SPOKEN BY THE PROPHET], They parted my garments . . ."

(6) Mark 14:68. "But he denied. . . . And he went out into the porch; [AND THE COCK CREW]."

(7) Hebrews 7:21. "the Lord sware and will not repent, Thou art a priest forever [AFTER THE ORDER OF MELCHISEDEC]"

22. Omission of the Personality of Satan.

Luke 4:8. "Jesus answered and said unto him, [GET THEE BEHIND ME, SATAN] for it is written, . . ."

23. Omission of Separation from Unbelievers and False Teachers.

1 Timothy 6:5. "supposing that gain is godliness: [FROM SUCH WITHDRAW THYSELF]"

These above-mentioned verses of Scripture, with the omissions made in them by "B" and "Aleph" and their allies, together with many of the English versions and perversions based upon them, speak for themselves. Anyone who knows elementary Bible doctrine will be aware of the seriousness of many of these additions, omissions, or changes in the text. There are undoubtedly many more examples which could be quoted, but these are suggestive. It would be a profitable study to point out sometime all 5000 to 6000 changes which have been made by these heretical "B" and "Aleph" manuscripts when set over against the Greek New Testament followed by the KJB.

For more information on the doctrinal errors of these false Greek texts and English versions, you should get Dr. Jack Moorman's book. He has compiled 356 doctrinal passages where "B" and "Aleph" contain heresy. This is found in his book, *Early Manuscripts and the Authorized Version--a Closer Look*. It is **B.F.T. #1825 @ $15.00 +S&H**. I have selected 158 of these 356 doctrinal passages and explained their doctrinal errors in detail in my book, *Defending the King James Bible*, 5th printing hardback, Chapter V, pp. 131-183. This is **B.F.T. #1594-P**.

E. Conclusions About These Verses Which Are Omitted in the "B" and "Aleph" Alexandrian Family of Manuscripts. There are a few things which might be said concerning these preceding verses from the Bible which are left out of or omitted from "B" or "Aleph" families of Greek texts, and in many of our English translations.

1. The Omissions are DEFINITELY of a Doctrinal Nature And Involve Key New Testament Doctrines, Especially Involving Christology and Soteriology. The number of them and the nature of the omissions cannot be passed off as being caused by pure chance. Someone who believed in the heresies of the omissions and who was in a position to corrupt the manu- scripts of the "B" and "Aleph" allies along these lines did so. And the simple, Bible-believing Christians knew this had happened, and hence shunned these false manuscripts, copying only the Traditional Text which was pure. This explains the presence of 99% of the Greek manuscripts we have today being in the Traditional Received Text.

2. The Omissions are NOT Backed up by the Traditional, Received Text in the Greek, Consisting of the Vast Majority of Extant Manuscripts. These corruptions occur only in the manuscripts represented by "B" and "Aleph," the corrupted texts, and are not in the *Textus Receptus* texts of the New Testament.

3. Our Strong Objection to these OMISSIONS Should Not be Lessened Merely Because Other Verses in the New Testament Might Teach These Doctrines Elsewhere. It is a serious problem to omit vital doctrines of the New Testament by means of heretics who willfully corrupted or changed the New Testament Greek texts, regardless of whether or not these doctrines are repeated in other books. So far as the corrupter might have known, the portion before him which he corrupted and changed by omission may have been the only place in the New Testament that contained this doctrine. He might not have had the entire New Testament in his possession. He might have thought he was rooting out entirely from the N.T. the various doctrines he omitted from the Sacred text. Remember Hort's "thorough scheme" and his changing of a doctrine by changing here a little and there a little?

> *How vastly different are the errors of the Revised!* [in contrast to the good work of the Received Text and the KJB]. *They are the product of a well-laid, designing scheme to incorporate in the text the theology of the revisers. Westcott, writing to Hort before the committee was under way* [that is, the Revision Committee of the ERV of 1881], *rejoiced that the future chairman, Dr. Ellicott, was "quite capable of accepting heartily and adopting personally a thorough scheme." And when the new book was published, Bishop Westcott recommended it to the Bible student, because the profound effect on a doctrine was produced by changing "here a little, there a little." He*

clearly convicted the Revised version of being the product of a design-
ing scheme with an ulterior purpose. [Dr. David Otis Dr. Fuller,
Which Bible, pp. 214-215]
There is no telling what further omissions might be seen in the 20th century as the
Greek texts are corrupted by omission. This has been done often without any
textual justification, but accepting mere "conjectural emendation." at will. It is
sometimes done without even so much as a footnote to indicate it.

**4. Though the Versions and Transla-
tions Listed on Previous Pages of the Paper Did
Not All Omit These Verses 100%, What is to
Prevent Even the Most Conservative Text of
These 44 Translations to Omit ALL of Them in
Later Editions?** It will not suffice to content ourselves in the fact that
Wuest's Expanded Translation, for example, omitted 88% of these 162 verses [or
portions of them] and printed 12% of them, rather than omitting 100% of them.
Even though Wuest was a conservative theologian, there is nothing to prevent
later editions of his work from omitting 100% of these 162 verses (or portions
thereof] should they so desire. The issues involved in "B" and "Aleph"
corruptions must be exposed for all to see before it is too late. There were very
good reasons for the 99% of our extant Greek manuscripts representing the
Traditional-Received Text to reject the follies of "B" and "Aleph" and their
family of corrupted texts. Doctrine is one very good reason.

**5. There Must Be a Clear Distinction Be-
tween the Quality of a Translation from Hebrew and Greek into English and the Hebrew or
Greek TEXT Which was Used to Make the
Translation.** Some of the translations listed above, in this section, may
be better than others, BUT their Greek Text from which they translated is the "B"
and "Aleph" corrupted text, for the most part, under the influence of apostates
Westcott and Hort and company. This is sad indeed.

CHAPTER VII
CONCLUDING REMARKS

A few concluding remarks will be added here in order to sum up a few matters of importance.

I. We Must Revive the Hebrew and Greek Received Texts

Before the many Greek and Hebrew manuscripts go into popular eclipse, we must continue to revive and MAKE AVAILABLE THE RECEIVED HEBREW AND GREEK TEXTS. The margins should be wide enough to make it possible to indicate the various changes that Westcott and Hort made to the *Textus Receptus* Greek text. Dr. Frederick Scrivener has done this in the past, and Dr. Kirk DiVietro is working on bringing this up-to-date in computer format so it can be printed and made available in clear format.

II. The Presence of the United Bible Society's Greek Text Argues all the More to Re-Print, Re-Publish and Widely Distribute the Greek Received Text

The United Bible Society's use of "B" and "Aleph" after the Westcott and Hort tradition, makes it all the more essential to keep in distribution a RECEIVED TEXT which represents 99% of our extant Greek manuscripts today. [The same goes for an uncorrupted MASORETIC HEBREW OLD TESTAMENT TEXT as well, for the same reasons.] We cannot fight the translations themselves alone, but must come to grips with the TEXTS which are used in the Hebrew and Greek, and make certain they are true to the *Textus Receptus* New Testament and the Masoretic Hebrew text underlying the King James Bible.

III. The Time Has Not Come to Tear the King James Bibles From Every Fundamentalist Pulpit and Pew in America!

We must continue to keep firm the Hebrew and Greek texts that underlie the King James Bible. These texts have been seriously eroded for decades, even among the so-called fundamentalists of our day. This must come to a halt. There must also be a renewed stand for the King James Bible on which these original language texts are based. Only then can we come to grips with the issues which make for MODERNISM, LIBERALISM, HERESY, AND APOSTASY. We must continue to battle other versions which have inferior Hebrew and Greek texts, inferior translators, inferior technique of translation, and inferior theology.

INDEX OF CERTAIN WORDS AND PHRASES

INDEX OF SCRIPTURE REFERENCES

About the Author

The author of this book, Dr. D. A. Waite, received a B.A. (Bachelor of Arts) in classical Greek and Latin from the University of Michigan in 1948, a Th.M. (Master of Theology), with high honors, in New Testament Greek Literature and Exegesis from Dallas Theological Seminary in 1952, an M.A. (Master of Arts) in Speech from Southern Methodist University in 1953, a Th.D. (Doctor of Theology), with honors, in Bible Exposition from Dallas Theological Seminary in 1955, and a Ph.D. in Speech from Purdue University in 1961. He holds both New Jersey and Pennsylvania teacher certificates in Greek and Language Arts.

He has been a teacher in the areas of Greek, Hebrew, Bible, Speech, and English for over thirty-five years in nine schools, including one junior high, one senior high, three Bible institutes, two colleges, two universities, and one seminary. He served his country as a Navy Chaplain for five years on active duty; pastored three churches; was Chairman and Director of the Radio and Audio-Film Commission of the American Council of Christian Churches; since 1971, has been Founder, President, and Director of THE BIBLE FOR TODAY; since 1978, has been President of the DEAN BURGON SOCIETY; since 1998, has been Pastor of THE BIBLE FOR TODAY BAPTIST CHURCH with his sermons and other messages heard daily all over the world on www.Bible ForToday. org by means of the internet; has produced over 900 other studies, books, cassettes, or VCR's on various topics; and is heard on both a five-minute daily and thirty-minute weekly radio program IN DEFENSE OF TRADITIONAL BIBLE TEXTS. Dr. and Mrs. Waite have been married since 1948; they have four sons, one daughter, and, at present, eight grandchildren.

Order Blank (p. 1)

Name:_____

Address:_____

City & State:_____Zip:_____

Credit Card #:_____Expires:_____

[ ] Send *The Case for the King James Bible* by DAW ($7 +S&H) A perfect bound book, 112 pages in length.

[ ] Send *Foes of the King James Bible Refuted* by DAW ($9 +$4 S&H) A perfect bound book, 164 pages in length.

[ ] Send *The Revision Revised* by Dean Burgon ($25 + $4) A hardback book, 640 pages in length.

[ ] Send *The Last 12 Verses of Mark* by Dean Burgon ($15+$4) A perfect bound paperback book 400 pages in length.

[ ] Send *The Traditional Text* hardback by Burgon ($16 + $4)

[ ] Send *Summary of Traditional Text* by Dr. Waite ($3 + $2)

[ ] Send *Summary of Causes of Corruption*, DAW ($3+2 S&H)

[ ] Send *Causes of Corruption* hardback by Burgon ($15 + $4)

[ ] Send *Inspiration and Interpretation*, Dean Burgon ($25+$4)

[ ]Send *Contemporary Eng. Version Exposed*, DAW ($3+$2)

[ ] Send the "DBS Articles of Faith & Organization" (N.C.)

[ ] Send Brochure #1: "1000 Titles Defending KJB/TR"(N.C.)

Send or Call Orders to:
THE BIBLE FOR TODAY
900 Park Ave., Collingswood, NJ 08108
Phone: 856-854-4452; FAX:--2464; Orders: 1-800 JOHN 10:9

Order Blank (p. 2)

Name:_____

Address:_____

City & State:_____Zip:_____

Credit Card#:_____Expires:_____

Other Materials on the KJB & T.R.

[ ] Send *Westcott & Hort's Greek Text & Theory Refuted by Burgon's Revision Revised--Summarized* by Dr. D. A. Waite ($3.00 + $3 S&H)

[ ] Send *Defending the King James Bible* by Dr.Waite $12+$4 A hardback book, indexed with study questions.

[ ] Send *Guide to Textual Criticism* by Edward Miller ($7 + $4)

[ ] Send *Heresies of Westcott & Hort* by Dr. Waite ($3+$3)

[ ] Send *Westcott's Denial of Resurrection*, Dr. Waite ($4+$3)

[ ] Send *Four Reasons for Defending KJB* by DAW ($2+$3)

[ ] Send *Vindicating Mark 16:9-20* by Dr. Waite ($3 + $3)

[ ] Send *Dean Burgon's Confidence in KJB* by DAW ($3+$3)

[ ] Send *Readability of A.V. (KJB)* by D. A. Waite, Jr. ($5 + $3)

[ ] Send *NIV Inclusive Language Exposed* by DAW ($4+$3)

[ ] Send *23 Hours of KJB Seminar (4 videos) by DAW ($50.00)*

Send or Call Orders to:
THE BIBLE FOR TODAY
900 Park Ave., Collingswood, NJ 08108
Phone: 856-854-4452; FAX:--2464; Orders: 1-800 JOHN 10:9
E-Mail Orders: BFT@BibleForToday.org; Credit Cards OK

Order Blank (p. 3)

Name:_____

Address:_____

City & State:_____Zip:_____

Credit Card#:_____Expires:_____

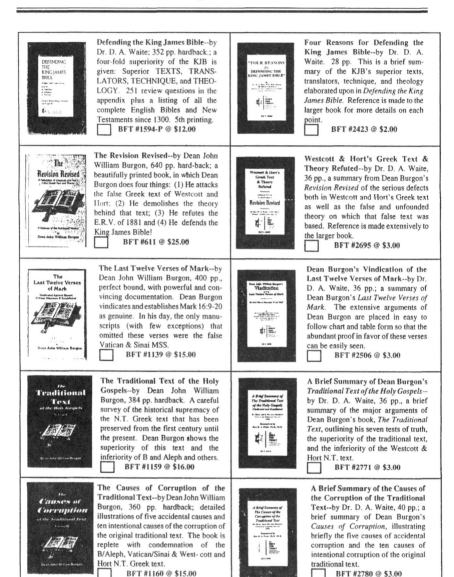

Defending the King James Bible--by Dr. D. A. Waite; 352 pp. hardback.; a four-fold superiority of the KJB is given: Superior TEXTS, TRANS-LATORS, TECHNIQUE, and THEO-LOGY. 251 review questions in the appendix plus a listing of all the complete English Bibles and New Testaments since 1300. 5th printing.
☐   BFT #1594-P @ $12.00

Four Reasons for Defending the King James Bible--by Dr. D. A. Waite. 28 pp. This is a brief summary of the KJB's superior texts, translators, technique, and theology elaborated upon in *Defending the King James Bible*. Reference is made to the larger book for more details on each point.
☐   BFT #2423 @ $2.00

The Revision Revised--by Dean John William Burgon, 640 pp. hard-back; a beautifully printed book, in which Dean Burgon does four things: (1) He attacks the false Greek text of Westcott and Hort; (2) He demolishes the theory behind that text; (3) He refutes the E.R.V. of 1881 and (4) He defends the King James Bible!
☐   BFT #611 @ $25.00

Westcott & Hort's Greek Text & Theory Refuted--by Dr. D. A. Waite, 36 pp., a summary from Dean Burgon's *Revision Revised* of the serious defects both in Westcott and Hort's Greek text as well as the false and unfounded theory on which that false text was based. Reference is made extensively to the larger book.
☐   BFT #2695 @ $3.00

The Last Twelve Verses of Mark--by Dean John William Burgon, 400 pp., perfect bound, with powerful and convincing documentation. Dean Burgon vindicates and establishes Mark 16:9-20 as genuine. In his day, the only manuscripts (with few exceptions) that omitted these verses were the false Vatican & Sinai MSS.
☐   BFT #1139 @ $15.00

Dean Burgon's Vindication of the Last Twelve Verses of Mark--by Dr. D. A. Waite, 36 pp.; a summary of Dean Burgon's *Last Twelve Verses of Mark*. The extensive arguments of Dean Burgon are placed in easy to follow chart and table form so that the abundant proof in favor of these verses can be easily seen.
☐   BFT #2506 @ $3.00

The Traditional Text of the Holy Gospels--by Dean John William Burgon, 384 pp. hardback. A careful survey of the historical supremacy of the N.T. Greek text that has been preserved from the first century until the present. Dean Burgon shows the superiority of this text and the inferiority of B and Aleph and others.
☐   BFT #1159 @ $16.00

A Brief Summary of Dean Burgon's *Traditional Text of the Holy Gospels*--by Dr. D. A. Waite, a brief summary of the major arguments of Dean Burgon's book, *The Traditional Text*, outlining his seven tests of truth, the superiority of the traditional text, and the inferiority of the Westcott & Hort N.T. text.
☐   BFT #2771 @ $3.00

The Causes of Corruption of the Traditional Text--by Dean John William Burgon, 360 pp. hardback; detailed illustrations of five accidental causes and ten intentional causes of the corruption of the original traditional text. The book is replete with condemnation of the B/Aleph, Vatican/Sinai & West-cott and Hort N.T. Greek text.
☐   BFT #1160 @ $15.00

A Brief Summary of the Causes of the Corruption of the Traditional Text--by Dr. D. A. Waite, 40 pp.; a brief summary of Dean Burgon's *Causes of Corruption*, illustrating briefly the five causes of accidental corruption and the ten causes of intentional corruption of the original traditional text.
☐   BFT #2780 @ $3.00

☐ **King James Bible Seminar Videos--Using 450 Transparencies FOUR, 6-hour Videos @ $45 + $5 S&H**

Foes of the King James Bible Refuted--by Dr. D. A. Waite , 158 pp.; a refutation of six leading foes of the KJB taken from the television script of the John Ankerberg program. The arguments are as old as the Westcott and Hort errors. They deserve clear answers and receive them in this booklet.

☐ BFT #2777 @ $9.00

The Comparative Readability of the Authorized Version--by Mr. D. A. Waite, Jr., 84 pp.; an objective, computer generated comparison of the readability of seven versions: KJB, ASV, RSV, NASV, NIV, NKJV, & NRSV. The King James Bible wins in read- ability in most categories based on current readability formulas.

☐ BFT #2671 @ $5.00

The Theological Heresies of Westcott and Hort--by Dr. D. A. Waite, 52 pp.; 125 direct quotations from three of Bishop Westcott's books and two of Professor Hort's books, showing their apostasy in all ten areas of theological thought. Don't believe those who tell you they were "conservative" theologians!

☐ BFT #595 @ $4.00

Bishop B. F. Westcott's Clever Denial of Christ's Bodily Resurrection--by Dr. D. A. Waite, 56 pp.; an analysis of two of Westcott's books on the resurrection of Christ showing clearly his heretical denial of Christ's **bodily** resurrection. He also denies Christ's **bodily** ascension and **bodily** second coming. Beware!

☐ BFT #1131 @ $4.00

Dean Burgon's Confidence in the King James Bible-- by Dr. D. A. Waite, 36 pp.; an answer to the lie of James White that Dean Burgon would not use ONLY the King James Bible. The booklet is replete with quotations from Dean Burgon's *Revision Revised* in which he defends the KJB forcefully and accurately!

☐ BFT #2591 @ $3.00

The Paraphrased Perversion of the Bible--Analysis of the Living Version N.T. by Dr. Gene Nowlin, 344 pp. perfect bound; a detailed analysis from a theological and translational standpoint of the *Living Version New Testament*. This should be given to those who still think there is spiritual value in the LV.

☐ BFT #127 @ $9.00

A Brief Analysis of the NIV Inclusive Language Edition ("NI-VILE)"--by Dr. D. A. Waite, 56 pp.; In spite of the plan of the NIV to go gender-inclusive and then the withdrawl of that plan, the NIV has published in England such an edition. 136 examples of faithless treatment of God's Words are given!

☐ BFT #2768 @ $4.00

The Contemporary English Version (CEV), An Antichrist Version (ACV)?--by Dr. D. A. Waite, 34 pp.; The latest perversion from the Amer-ican Bible Society is analyzed and condemned. 29 doctrinal words and 22 other important words have been dropped out of this CEV. Destined to be the pattern for the world!

☐ BFT #2721 @ $3.00

The Case for the King James Bible, A Summary of the Evidence and Argument--by Dr. D. A. Waite, 96 pp.; this booklet is a brief summary from three different books of the favorable evidence for the Hebrew and Greek texts that underlie the King James Bible. An update of the author's 1971 work.

☐ BFT #83 @ $7.00

The Textus Receptus Greek New Testament Underlying the KJB--printed by The Trinitarian Bible Society, 487 pp.; this is a reprint of Dr. Frederick Scrivener's Greek text which exactly underlies the King James Bible. It is based on Beza's 5th edition of 1598 and **should be** the basis for any New Testament translation in any language.

☐ BFT #471 @ $14.00

the
**BIBLE
FOR
TODAY**

900 Park Avenue
Collingswood, NJ 08108
Phone: 856-854-4452
www.BibleForToday.org

B.F.T. #83

ISBN #1-56848-011-3